Don't Be Needy
Be Succeedy

L. VAUGHAN SPENCER

Don't Be Needy
Be Succeedy

The A to Zee of Motivitality©

PROFILE BOOKS

First published in Great Britain in 2008 by
PROFILE BOOKS LTD
3a Exmouth House
Pine Street
London EC1R 0JH
www.profilebooks.com

A CIP catalogue record for this book is available from the British Library.

ISBN 978 1 84668 163 9

Text design by Sue Lamble

Typeset in Century by MacGuru Ltd
info@macguru.org.uk

Printed in the UK by CPI Bookmarque, Croydon, CR0 4TD

☆ *About the Author*

L. Vaughan Spencer was named the 2004 Business Speaker of the Year for Bedfordshire and Hertfordshire and came twelfth in the Northern Hemisphere Motivator of the Year (Under-40 Middleweight Section). He is Business Ambassador for the South-East England Tree Fellowship, editor-at-large of *Success & Succeediness* and is the Kall-Kwik Visiting Professor of Succeedership at the University of the Isle of Wight. He is a member of the board of governors of Sky-brook Primary School in Stevenage.

He is the chief executive of the L. Vaughan Spencer Foundation, a not-for-much-profit organisation dedicated to its betterment, and of Succeeder Solutions, which provides 'bespoke solutions to tricky problems'. He is chair of the SUCCEEDER INSTITUTE, a think tank on important things which is trying to advise the government. He is considered one of the world's leading TRENDOLOGISTS. Having looked at Generation X, then Generation Y, he is firmly focused on the prospects for Generation Z. What comes after that remains unclear.

He is a global force and helped organise the famous Motiv-8 Event in July 2005, held near Wembley and at locations across the world and Hertfordshire. Leading lights in the personal growth industry attended and so did someone from the European Union. In 2006 he was appointed a Senior Fellow at the Advanced Seminar of Succeederology (ASS), which is now offering a new course, 'The Two-Minute MBA'.

As one of the UK's leading thinkers (he has been acknowledged as one of the top ten thousand most influential people on management issues in the Home Counties), he does a lot of thinking, often about leadership, and is in demand internationally as an inspiring speaker, renowned for his passion and dress sense. His insightful and skilful story-telling means he can make the big picture seem even bigger. He sits on the European Cheese Council and plays tennis.

L. Vaughan Spencer was recently awarded the Gold Star Lifetime Achievement Award by the Personal Development Association of Newfoundland for his services to humanity and sales of his videos. He has been married and lives in the Succeeder Triangle (see below) not far from London Luton Airport.

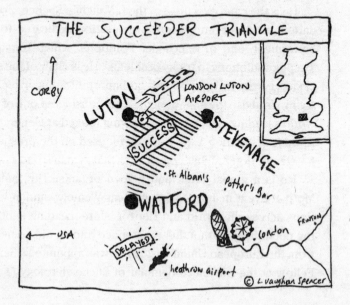

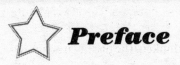 # *Preface*

by Nigel Venture, Chief Executive of Stevenage Enterprise Body

When I was asked to write this preface I was very pleased. Mr Spencer has run several of our in-house 'Motivitality Days'. Each one has had a powerful effect on the team – I can see everyone doing lots of P-MOVES, which cheers me no end. Because of various commitments, I haven't been able to attend one myself, but I've promised that next time I will, though quite when that will be is not clear at the moment, with the budget cuts that we are having to make. Mr Spencer has been very understanding and offered to reduce his fee. I envisage that we will be able to undertake this meaningful and important team-building event (which I am sure will lead to lots of creativising, as Mr Spencer promises) in Q4 of next year, probably instead of the Christmas party. There is no question that there can be only one man for the job – L. Vaughan Spencer. I am writing this preface with one of his SUCCEEDER pens, and there's no question that it's all the better for it. I fully endorse this book. I don't often read books, but this one certainly looks good from the outside. Enjoy!

⭐ *Introduction*

'GET READY – FOR THE RIDE OF YOUR LIFE!' says L. Vaughan Spencer

Julius Caesar was an early Succeeder. Remember his catch-phrase? *Veni, vidi, succeedi* … I came, I saw, I succeeded. I'm a Succeeder in a long line of Succeeders. Caesar, Abraham Lincoln, Tim Henman and Phil Collins – all undoubtedly used my methods. They may not have realised it at the time, but they did! I have been working with many organisations and individuals (including some celebrities and minor members of the royal family that I can't mention), introducing my Succeeder© programmes. It's about embedding cogno-sensual learnings and initiating proactive mindful Motivitality©. It don't come cheap. But try a preliminary exercise right now *for free*. Look into a mirror and say, 'I am Succeedy©' seven times. Feels good, doesn't it? Real good! (You can buy a Succeeder Mirror from the online Succeeder Store for £8.99 at thesucceeder.com.)

Think of this book as *The Da Vinci Code* of motivational business. By that I mean not only should it sell lots of copies and be made into a film starring Tom Hanks (not with that hair, anyway. And I will play me) but that it uncovers a conspiracy. The conspiracy is that for too long you have been allowed to fail. Who's been keeping you down? YOURSELF! That's right. It's time to fight your inner demons and overcome that negative inner dialogue that keeps telling you you're not good enough. Can you hear that voice saying, 'Ooh, there's no way you can be rich and successful. People don't like you. Even your partner doesn't really?' Well, by the time you've finished reading this book, that won't happen again. If it does, you may need to go on my Succeeder Failure course. I offer a 10 per cent discount for those who come back twice.

This book will enhance your personal and business life. Because, of course, business is personal, isn't it? Most management writers have overlooked the basics of business – what you look like and how you feel – in their rush to analyse facts and figures and introduce models (and I'm talking paradigms here – not size-zero lovelies!). I look deeper than the bottom line. I see beyond the numbers. All of my work is based on a rigorous analysis – apart from where it's easier not to.

Not everyone is born with Succeediness but it can be trained in even the most surprising cases (at the right price). Look at the table below and see on which side of the divide you fall.

Succeedy	Needy
EQ	B&Q
Power Point	Power Nap
Flip Chart	Flip Flop
Intent	In a Tent

This book follows the structure of the British alphabet. It is the alpha to omega of Motivitality©, a route map to success; the Alphabet of Achievement for the Alpha Male (or Alpha Female – let's not forget how many of them there are now!). So you can read it all the way through or dip into certain bits. This book goes from A to Zee, but I know life doesn't always follow that route. Maybe A comes before B comes before C (you eat an Apple before a Banana and then some Cheese), but oftentimes an R comes *before* an M: Romance comes before Marriage. Then you have D for Divorce.

There are plenty of business books out there. One I particularly recommend is by my old mucker Francis Babbage – or Frankie B, as he affects to be known, prancing on to the stage to the sounds of Sister Sledge's 'Frankie'. Who could fail to be moved by his book *Change Your Life in Seven Words – Now!*? Or the follow-up, *Change Your Life in These Seven Words*, which, despite being virtually the same, still did so well in the charts? His face was everywhere, and the books gave him the chance to host his own TV Show, *Life-Changer!*, which so many of us enjoyed, and which certainly didn't deserve the negative coverage I kept seeing whenever I opened a newspaper.

This book is different. And it's different from all those ones about cheese by American writers which followed on from *Who Moved My Cheese-Burger?* – my own radical treatise on supply chains. First there was *Good to Grate* by Collin Jims, which changed the way so many CEOs look at top-slicing. And who hasn't gone and bought several copies of Peter Toms's wonderful *In Search of Emmental* – one man's quest to find holiness in the business world? For more on these fascinating parallels, see the entry under CHEESE & BUSINESS.

Other books I recommend include Taylor David's two excellent works, *The Knackered Leader* and *The Neutered Coach* (introducing the concept of Neutered Language©, a non-gender-specific language for the sensitive coach of either sex), Malcolm Wellglad's *The Point of Tipping* (a passionate case for great customer service) and its follow-ups, first on organisational creativity, *Blank*, and then *Bling* (on the use of jewellery in the boardroom), and finally Charles Hungry's *The Handy Spirit*, a radical defence of the use of vodka in corporate strategy.

But remember – the more copies of this book you buy, the more successful you will be. Look at this graph:

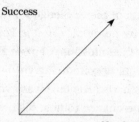

I hope that, like my other nineteen books, it will be available across the globe. For example, one of my latest, *The Seven Hobbies of Highly Effective People*, has just been translated into North Korean, and also Itakabi, a little-known language spoken only by a hill tribe of forty-six CEOs in the Peruvian Andes.

Treat this book as a friend. Keep in touch with it. When stuck in a tricky situation, I know it will help you to ask, 'What would L-Vo do?' So use this book as a guide. You're on the front line. I may be busy with other clients, or sunning myself in Morocco with a lady friend. You're in the driving seat. Sure, I've given you a map, but you've got to be your own sat-nav!

But keep in touch with me anyway. You can reach me via thesucceeder.com. You can sign up for a Virtual Vaughan

Session for just £84. Send me a photo and I might even ring you for some intensive one-on-one. And buy another book for a friend. Don't keep it secret. Succeediness is not a zero-sum game. There's plenty to go around, although buying a second (and even third) book for yourself may just ensure you have a bit more than the next guy. Better still, sign up for a Succeeder Weekend Workshop. We hold them regularly in Watford, at the Ramada Jarvis, a delightful luxury-style hotel with the Arts Bar Café 'n' Grill and the Sebastian Coe Health Park.

There are plenty of books out there that encourage thought or talk. Not this one. It's about doing. Or 'Doin' the do' – as Betty Boo so rightly said. It's not about talk-talk. The advice in this book is all do-do. I don't apologise for that.

The Advice in This Book Is All Do-Do!

A word of warning. There has been some coverage of a scurrilous website, succeedernot.com, which details the gripes of some toxic folk who just wouldn't allow themselves to be swept along in the Succeeder Stream. They stayed in the River of Rage and my first ex-wife seems to be prominent among them. The fact that they idolise Frankie B, the so-called Life-Changer, means I pity them all the more.

L-v-o-e
L-Vo xxxx

The L. Vaughan Spencer Foundation
Luton, England
November 2008

Disclaimer

If you find any similarity to yourself, then go ahead and sue me. Better still, change yourself, so that you aren't recognisable. If this book doesn't make you a Succeeder, it's your fault, not mine. I've done my bit.

I am grateful to various people who have read early drafts of this book. Most especially, my editor, Ned. The book was not written in the easiest of circumstances, with various technical and personal issues impeding my ability to complete it on time, but Ned has always been totally firm – reminding me that the advance would only be fully paid on publication. If any errors remain, the fault, of course, lies entirely with him.

Absenteeism

When people don't turn up to work. Often confused with 'working from home' (as I am today!), which is altogether different. Absenteeism may often be caused by people feeling *under-motivitalised* at work. So it's important to make people feel happy at work – and appreciation has never been more vital than in today's fast-moving business environment (FMBE). When I go into a company, I often hold an APPRECIATION HOUR, where we really take time to appreciate one another, through talking, touching and SUCCEEDER SILENCE. Appreciation is but one of the many dishes on the menu in the tapas bar of LEADERSHIP. However, if you are feeling underappreciated at work, then call in the SAS (Succeeder Action Squad). I may be able to come round and give you your own private MOTIVITALITY moment and in no time at all you'll want to get back to the office. Please send photo to me at my Luton HQ. Of course, there are some people whose absence is much appreciated. Absenteeism may well make the heart grow fonder.

Accreditation

Where something is approved by another institution. All SUC-CEEDER courses have been fully accredited by the Kentucky College of Accreditation and the Succeeder Institute and could well count towards your Continuing Succeedy Development (CSD).

[*Ned*: I think it's useful where possible to put these things in context. I will mention Succeeder products so as to illustrate a point, not just to drive traffic to the website thesucceeder.com, where special deals are available on Succeeder courses and merchandise, and there is a quiz where they can win things. So don't cut them please.]

Adam

I like to think of Adam as 'The First Businessman'. The clear lesson from his business case is that his Procurement Manager (Eve) did not carry out full due diligence on their fruit supplier (a serpent), which led to complications in issues such as HEALTH AND SAFETY, CSR and CORPORATE GOVERNANCE. Their business never really recovered and we are still living with the consequences today. They ate from the tree of Right and Wrong, always a mistake in the Garden of Business. So the Big Guy upstairs changed their terms. In many ways, I see myself as an Adam for the modern age, the First Man of MOTIVITALITY, if you will. Right now there isn't an Eve, but I might be prepared to donate a rib in exceptional circumstances.

Adam Smith

Named after the first businessman, Adam, ex-husband of Eve. He was Scottish (from Kirkcaldy – home of linoleum) and got lucky with his second book, *The Wealth of Nations*, in 1776, the first being the less well-known *The Leech and Potato Diet*. Having read a summary of his work on the net, I found that his big thing was the 'invisible hand' of market forces, echoed years later in the Genesis song, 'Invisible Touch', sung by Phil Collins, which pretty much nailed the basis of laissez-faire market capitalism:

> *She seems to have an invisible touch yeah*
> *She reaches in, and grabs right hold of your heart*
> *She seems to have an invisible touch yeah*
> *It takes control and slowly tears you apart.*

It sure does! The market is a bewitching lady, an enchantress, with her obedient sirens – Supply and Demand. That's why I sometimes have to drop my prices. Yet still Nigel Venture is trying to get me down below fifty quid, with Succeeder Pens thrown in. I guess you don't get to be head of Stevenage Enterprise Body without a steely nose for negotiation.

[*Ned*: I presume you will be paying for permission on the above song extract? Looks like I will have to use most of my advance on a new computer. I got my nephew, Liam, round this morning to come and look at it and apparently I'm in the Stone Age, or the one before. And it looks like I might have to fork out for an agency temp soon. My assistant, Nikki, isn't replying to my texts.]

Advanced Seminar on Succeederology (ASS)

A standing committee of the great and the good in Luton and beyond, attempting to bring together all sorts of disciplines – sociology, social psychology, neurology, biology and tennis.

Increasingly different disciplines are coming together these days. Business (Biz) is realising that the Personal Development (PerDev) world has plenty to say to it. This book is creating a new genre, PerDevBiz (PDB), for everyone who's in the PDB market – which, let's face it, is everybody in the world.

Advertising

How do I advertise my work? I put an ad in the *Luton News* and the *Dunstable Gazette*. They're sister papers, so can offer a really good deal for the two. However, mostly I publicise through personal and media appearances. For example, on the Big L, Luton's local radio station, I host *The Succeeder Hour*, sponsored by Luton Futon, where 'A Good Night's Sleep Really Does Come Cheap'. It's an interactive show. People ring in with their issues and opinions. There's a fascinating bunch of people out there between 3 and 4 on a Tuesday morning. Occasionally, I co-host with Les Goodhall, former soccer player with Luton Town Football Club, though it has to be said that 3 a.m. is not his best time.

See also DADVERTISING.

Airport

A great example of creative business. Especially (says a cynical friend of mine, Frederick) in selling unwanted gifts to businessmen or women who are feeling guilty. Teddies, jam, perfume, infant sports uniforms and giant chocolate landmarks are all purchased for ungrateful family members. Sometimes I need to go to an airport for business. For example, I had a hand in the customer service training leading up to the opening of Terminal 5 at London's other airport, Heathrow.

One time I got upgraded to Business Class. (Normally I prefer to fly Economy so I can mingle with the real people.) There's a lounge you can go where you don't have to pay for the newspapers or the food (you can really 'Max the Buffet'). I find it fascinating just to chat to people at travel hubs like airports, taxi ranks and bus stations, to find out about them and their issues. I've made many great friends this way and I know that several of them have been moved to take a really hard look at themselves and their lives. For example, after I spoke to one guy at Luton for just a few minutes, he said he suddenly felt the need to go to the airport chapel.

In many ways, life is like air travel. Only some are in the Executive Club. If you go far enough, you get rewarded, either by discounted flights or by getting 15 per cent off at luggage suppliers. Are your cabin doors to manual? Have you stowed your tray table of torment? How much emotional baggage are you carrying? Are you careful when undoing the overhead lockers? Things may have moved during the flight and could fall on your head.

Alphabet Arithmetic

How do you get more than 110 per cent in business? Here's something to make you think. If:

A B C D E F G H I J K L M N O P Q R S T U V W X Y Z
is represented as
1 2 3 4 5 6 7 8 9 10 11 12 13 14 15 16 17 18 19 20 21 22 23 24 25 26

then L-U-C-K = 12 + 21 + 3 + 11 = 47%

and K-N-O-W-L-E-D-G-E = 11 + 14 + 15 + 23 + 12 + 5 + 4 + 7 + 5 = 96%

and H-A-R-D-W-O-R-K = 8 + 1 + 18 + 4 + 23 + 15 + 18 + 11 = 98%

but …

L-V-A-U-G-H-A-N-S-P-E-N-C-E-R = 166%

and, not surprisingly, F-R-A-N-K-I-E-B = 6 + 18 + 1 + 14 + 11 + 9 + 5 + 2 = 66% (a whole hundred less than me!)

This helped me to come up with the ancient art of SPELLOL-OGY. And remember, whatever you do, never give less than 166 per cent!

Alphabet Diet

The SUCCEEDER needs to be aware of what he (or she) is eating. So I do Nutritional Counselling. To be a SUCCEEDER you have to eat food that is harmonious for you. You've heard about all the different diets on offer – low-carb, no-carb, bi-carb, whatever. They're all rubbish. Ditch the Dumb Diets! Forget the Fads! Listen to L-Vo. It's simple and it works. You must eat only food that begins with the same letter as your name. This is the Alphabet Diet. This is SPELLOLOGY applied to food and it will help you give 166 per cent even on a Tuesday.

So, for example, I am L-Vo. In English my first initial is L. Hence, I eat lamb, leeks, lettuce (lamb's lettuce is doubly good), liver, lozenges, luxury mince pies from Marks & Spencer, and anything from Lebanon. But that may not work for you (unless your name begins with an L). One man's meat is another man's mackerel. I allowed my assistant, Nikki, to eat only nuts, noodles and Nestlé products.

You can change to a different initial every month. So next

month, I can eat things starting with V, then S the following month. You may want to bear this in mind when naming your children. And this might be a problem for people with only one name (for example, Pink, who was so keen to 'Get the party started').

See also Appendices for full list of applicable foods.

Alpha Male

The kind of guy who wants to finish first. He will do anything necessary to clamber his way to the top, so this is not necessarily a good label. I used to be an Alpha Male but I've moved on. Now I am an Alpha Romeo. The Alpha Female is like the Alpha Male but uses a broader, more sophisticated range of tools. The Alpha Male has much to learn from his female counterpart, in terms of dress, MOISTURISER and HAIR. There's also the Alfalfa Male – an Alpha Male who eats macrobiotically. I tried doing this but didn't like it much. I realised why later – I had to eat too many things not beginning with L.

Alumni

For those who have been on a Succeeder course, there is an Alumni Association, so you can keep in touch with others on the Succeeder path. There is a regular *Succeed-e-zine*, where you can keep up with L-Vo's latest exploits. And you get a badge. There are regular Alumni reunions, so don't ever feel you will be left behind. Though you will be if you don't join the Alumni Association (£39). Every month a lucky alumna (or alumnus)

[*Ned*: I'm not sure which is male and which is female. Can we make sure that we give more emphasis to the lady side of things here? I don't want to be seen as sexist!] is picked at random for a free coaching session with L-Vo himself. Please send photo.]

Anger

Getting so worked up you shout or hit something or someone or alternatively go very quiet and then shout or hit something or someone. Vital in today's fast-moving business environment (FMBE).

Are You Getting Hot Under the (White) Collar?

According to recent research from Professor Barnaby Krench of Succeeder Lab, 73 per cent of us spend most of our time at work angry. What makes us so angry?

Colleagues	11%
Colleagues' clothes	5%
Boss	22%
Boss's clothes	*3%*
Boss moving the goalposts	*10%*
Not having any goalposts	*9%*
Computer	33%
Coffee machine	2%
Having to queue for lunch	4%
Somebody else's 'funny' ringtone	1%
Dearth of proper hand-drying facilities in the toilet either because the hand-dryer doesn't work or because there aren't enough paper towels or if there are they've all fallen on the floor	21%
World poverty	1%

Often the problem is not anger but the lack of a means for expressing it. With several organisations we have created a safe space for Holistic Howling. It's soundproofed (though 'thrash metal' music is piped in loudly), with punchbags laid on, as well as a facsimile of a computer terminal made of sponge that can be kicked around the room and a dartboard with a selection of photographs of company personnel that can be attached. (We also have an emergency supply of paper towels there for the 21 per cent who have a major issue with this.) If you find you need to visit you are allowed to go immediately, with no more explanation than, 'I need a Tantrum Trip.' You put a red Post-it note on your forehead and people must get out of your way. But you can stay no longer than three and a half hours, by which time it is hoped that the Monster Moment has passed and the meeting can resume – or, in a recent case with a client and me, the one-on-one ANGER MANAGEMENT session.

Anger Management

Have you thought about attending an Anger Management course or working with a coach on your anger? Notice I don't talk about anger reduction or getting rid of anger. Read my article in the *Journal of Anger Management* called 'Why Anger is Good' (though they did cut part of it, which pissed me off big time). Anger helps us prioritise and focus. Anger is perfectly natural and you don't get anywhere by denying it.

Accept Your Anger!

Embrace it, invite it in for a cup of tea and a bit of a chat. Feed and nourish it. Own it. Then let it go. Give it to someone else. Maybe someone in the lunch queue. Why not keep an Anger Diary? Write down what happened and how angry you got on a scale of nought to five. Looking through mine for today, I can see that I got tetchy over some stationery, irritated on the phone and frustrated with the television, for example. I've reached a score of 38 this morning but I'm hoping that once I've had breakfast things will calm down.

Animal Analysis

Business is like the animal world. There are so many parallel issues in wildlife and organisational life:

☆ Have I marked my territory?

☆ Who is the dominant one in the group?

☆ Will they share their food with me – or will they chase me away?

☆ Is it the mating season?

☆ Where can I get a drink?

☆ What's happening back at my nest – did I secure the entrance?

☆ Why am I being chased by a man with a big gun?

☆ What's that funny smell?

Following pioneering work by Professor Krench of Succeeder Lab, we have developed Animal Analysis© – or Anim-Alysis©. Do you recognise yourself and any of your office colleagues from this list? What kind of business animal are you?

Tortoise – slow but gets there in the end.

Chameleon – changes colours according to the situation.

Anteater – eats ants.

Elephant – never forgets anything and squashes anything in its path.

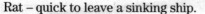

Rat – quick to leave a sinking ship.

Vulture – spots easy pickings once others have done the hard work.

Spider – good on the web.

Dolphin – highly intelligent, good at singing and can clean its own teeth.

Lion – king of the jungle with great hair.

Crow – moves only in straight lines.

Bull – not good in a china shop.

Skunk – smelly.

Zebra – Unlikely to be seen against black and white backgrounds.

Once you know which animal you are, unleash yourself! Make a pledge now! Here!

I promise to unleash the (insert animal here) .... in me.

Learn to work with your animal. Go and see one in the zoo. Look at how it goes about its business. Pick up some tips. One of my clients is a gibbon and he swings from shopping trolley to shopping trolley, making that characteristic cry in the morning to stake his territory.

See also DOLPHINS IN BUSINESS and ELEPHANT.

Appraisal

This meaningful ritual happens once a year, but ideally should happen each week. Yet so many businessfolk don't really know how to carry them out properly and gain from them. It's difficult to say if in the trad appraisal it's more painful for the appraiser or appraisee. It's ironic that the word 'praise' is embedded in it, since not much of that is involved.

For example, when I worked in a call centre (for research purposes) my appraisal after a day was 'not very good … finds it hard to work with other people … poor communication skills … brusque telephone manner … took far too long for lunch break'. What nonsense! And what use for going forward in full P-THINK mode?

There may be 360-degree feedback involved. That doesn't go far enough. The SUCCEEDER INSTITUTE offers some appraisal courses, entitled 'How to Give Appraisals', which teach my world-renowned 720-degree feedback technique. I come along to see how you give appraisals and teach you to become an Appraisals Appraiser. Appraisals Appraisers are continually appraised to make sure that they are fully apprised of their appraisal appraisals. But think of it differently. To App-raise is to Raise APP, a great Three-Letter Acronym or TLA …

Authentic   Personal   Power

We'll come to 'Authentic' in a bit and I can hardly wait! When getting ready to App-Raise someone, focus on how the experience can raise the APP for both of you! Just telling them what they've done wrong isn't going make it happen. Though, with Nikki, it has been necessary to point out areas of what I would call 'Challenge', where some work was necessary. Inviting her boyfriend into work during office hours did raise some issues, as did his non-adherence to the NO-SWEARING RULE.

Appreciation Hour

At the L. Vaughan Spencer Foundation, we always hold an Appreciation Hour, with some light gamelan (Indonesian percussion) music in the background. Nikki tends to arrive late, so it's often just me. At the moment she's not arriving at all.

[*Ned*: For the moment I'm having to be my own PA, which means fixing my own schedule, having to buy my own plane tickets etc. Luckily, my diary is fairly free at the moment and I'm not having to fly anywhere, though I have booked my usual Christmas trip to Norway.]

'The Appreciation Hour really changed the way we saw our work. The place really hasn't been the same since L-Vo came.'

Trolley Recovery Squad, Morrison's, Berkhamsted

Art Therapy

Vital in today's fast-moving business environment (FMBE). Isn't Art great? Pictures and sculpture and what-have-you. Some of the world's Great Artists have been really great. And then there are Artistes – using a broader notion of Art that includes writing, acting, film, dance, juggling and snooker. In many ways, I think of myself as the Martin Scorsese of Success, the Meryl Streep of MOTIVITALITY, the Cirque du Soleil of SUCCEEDEROLOGY or the John Virgo of NEW VIRILITY. So how do I use Art Therapy in my work? Sometimes when team-work, LEADERSHIP or strategy issues need unlocking, I just leave the senior management team alone with some clay and a gentle soundtrack from *Succeeder Relaxation Tape*, Volume 1, which features dolphins in mid-conversation. The results can be miraculous. What comes out of that kiln can be amazing. What comes out of the subsequent conversations always is. For example:

'I didn't like John but once I had finished my clay cat, I found it easier to ignore him.'

'By putting all of my hatred into that model of a giraffe I was able to forgive the one person I couldn't before – Sharon.'

'Sometimes, it's just the simple things. Like wear a smock if you don't want to get clay on your "hole-in-one" tie.'

Certainly Art Therapy has been very useful in my Personal Self-Enhancement work with the boys at Harpenden Young Offenders' Institution. They seemed to find it very therapeutic to draw pictures of me. Even though some of the drawings were less than flattering, I didn't mind, as it seemed to do the boys good.

Assertiveness

Vital in today's fast-moving business environment (FMBE). We respect people who assert. However, some people don't know where the line between assertiveness and aggression is. Here is a table that helps.

Assertive	Aggressive
Suit	Balaclava
Looking	Punching
Karaoke	Karate
Ribbing	Breaking ribs
Hospitality	Hospitalising
Coffee break	Leg break
Baseball analogy	Baseball bat
Knocking heads together	Knocking someone's head into a filing cabinet

Here's a rule of thumb:

Assert: Don't Hurt!

See also BAP SCALE.

Attitude Sickness

Like altitude sickness only with Attitude instead.

See also CEO.

Auntie Ambiguity

That funny old lady Auntie Ambiguity faces the businessperson day in and day out, along with her big bro, UNCLE UNCERTAINTY. Thing is, we can't predict the future. Any old fool can predict the past. We live in ambiguous times. Is this product going to save us or will it tank and bury the business? Should I hire this guy even though he has terrible dress sense? If I shout at this person, they might do the job better or they might hit me with a stapler. Ouch. Every day is a judgement call. Succeedership is all about making decisions and living or dying by them. The Clash understood ambiguity in that jeans commercial ...

> *Should I stay or should I go now?*
> *If I go there will be trouble;*
> *An' if I stay there will be double.*

Seems like a no-brainer. If you only want half the amount of trouble, then it's best to go. They worked their way through it. Have you?

Awayday

(US) *Retreat; also known as 'Off-Site'.*

The Succeeder and colleagues sometimes need to get away from the everyday environment to realise how much they really like each other. The day may involve some light-hearted TEAM-BUILDING activity, such as making you into two teams and pushing you out into a forest, armed only with guns that spray paint and can cause actual bodily harm if fired at close range. This really brings people together.

Aych-Are

I have recently returned from South America, where I was studying a primitive people, called the Aych-Are tribe. Little understood and distrustful of strangers, this bloodthirsty group has much to teach us about maintaining peak perform-ance. If anyone is found to be falling short, there's a strict procedure:

1. Verbal warning
2. Written warning
3. Access to top-class coaching on the issue concerned
4. Second written warning
5. Interview, with lawyer or responsible adult present
6. Death
7. Appeals process

However, they do their best to avoid poor performance by regular ceremonies, known as Ah-Weh-Daiz. They leave the safety of their village and travel medium to long distances to places lacking in all but the most basic of facilities for survival – food, drink and flip charts. The days are spent in long, demanding sessions during which only a few (never the wisest) speak at length with apparently no purpose. This is because the evenings are when what really matters most occurs. Sophisticated courtship displays and status rites are enacted around a sacred area known as the Ho-Telbar. Tribal members assume roles quite different from their everyday ones. Sacrifices take place, involving nudity, water, plant pots and sometimes even fire extinguishers. Normality only returns the following morning with the distribution of the holy chits known as the Bah-Beels, which have reduced grown men to quivering wrecks. Many leave these occasions broken and bloodied. But those who have endured them return strengthened by new knowledge (mostly of the intimate habits of the Elders), which means that one day they will take the place of these Elders. Like all primitive societies, myths build up about the feats achieved during the Ah-Weh-Daiz, but these bear little relation to reality.

B

As in Plan B. Sometimes you may want a Plan B in case Plan A doesn't work out. Some say that having a Plan B is actually showing that you aren't fully committed to Plan A, that you haven't really decided to go for it. I think the thing is to have a plan. Have you got a plan? What are you going to do with your life or business? It may well be it's actually your Plan C or even Plan Q, but make sure you have one.

Have a Plan!
Or You'll Carry the Can!

Write it down here:

MY PERSONAL PLAN IS

....

(sign your name here)

....

I know some of you may not want to write in a book. That's OK. I wrote this book and I give you permission.

'*I didn't have a plan. And now I do.*'

Curtis Lamp, Luton Learn-to-Drive

Babies

Babies are businesspeople of the future. They are simply developing their negotiating techniques. I'm currently rolling out some Toddler SUCCEEDER Workshops. But why wait till the little ones are born? Try some Pre-Birth Motivation©! One mother I know kept saying, 'You can do it!' to the lump in her tummy. You should see that kid now! He has his own online gaming empire at twelve.

Babies need a cuddle and so does anyone in business. I certainly do. It seems clear to me that Frankie B can only be such an empathetic guy because he did not have enough cuddles when he was young. It just seems a shame that he sought to make up that deficit from my now ex-wife. And, of course, when someone becomes a parent, their priorities change. Nikki, my assistant, who managed to persuade me that she needed maternity leave, still isn't back, and that baby left hospital well over two weeks ago!

Balloon of Destiny©

A physical way of expunging failure which is cheaper than a FIREWALK. The client simply blows into a balloon, but focuses on their failures, disappointments and flaws as they do so. Symbolically all these leave his or her body at this moment and enter the balloon. Then it is time to bring out the PIN OF DESTINY©. Simply burst the balloon and all those doubts, fears and failures will disappear. To use this technique, you just need to send me the £9.99 licence fee.*

For any coaches paying to copy this technique: Don't

stand too near when they burst the balloon. Some of their failures may land on you. This happened to me once. A particularly hapless individual let some of their negative ions fall on me and I had a terrible week thereafter. I had to take two days off, go for Deep Tissue Ego Massage with Cranston and his team of former paramilitaries, and burst my own balloon before I was able to rebalance my personal energy waves.

It should be simple, and highly effective. All it costs is the price of a balloon and a pin and of course the £9.99 licence fee (we can supply Pins of Destiny if required, but in minimum batches of a thousand. That represents a heck of a lot of failure for one person. Maybe a team can club together. Nice Buns Bakery did and their croissants are rising nicely now.)

See also FAILURE.

BAP Scale

Are you a bully or a pushover or something in between? Succeeder Solutions uses the BAP Scale:

Bully > Assertive > Pushover

Pushovers keep apologising, avoid eye contact, end up taking on too much and are generally doormats. *Bullies* blame everyone else, say horrid things and jostle you in the lift. *Assertives* respect others even if they have to disagree. Where are you on the BAP Scale?

I did hear the phrase 'Bully Broad' from an American the other day. This is a female bully. I have never met one myself. Apart from my sister.

Behaviour(s)

Research undertaken by Professor William Trankin of the Jimmy Connors Institute of Business in San Diego found that 76 per cent of what we do can be put down to our behaviours.

Are you aware of your behaviours? What are your behaviours? Do you have more than one? The worst thing I find is when people don't even realise how they are behaving. They have no self-awareness. I was constantly having to point out to Nikki that this was one of her challenges.

I am the Saviour of your Behaviour.
I can change the way you behave.
If you were a knave,
I can make you brave.
If you spend, then I'll help you save,
And find the success you ought to crave,
So you can go happily to your grave.

Belief

Do you believe in yourself? Of course not. And rightly so. But I believe in you, even though I've never met you. I believe you can do better. So much better. Are you ready to achieve? Then believe. Do you believe in God? Does God believe in you? Well, I do, and in many ways, it's much the same thing.

The first step to Achievement is Believement. Henry Ford said that if you believe you will fail or succeed then you are right both ways. And he built the Ford Fiesta.

Believe to Achieve!

In fact, if Henry Ford had followed the prevailing technology, he would have built a faster horse. That's how I feel in the world of MOTIVITALITY. Everyone else is trying to whip their donkey into shape, while I am offering a beautiful Saab of SUCCEEDINESS©, a Volvo of Vitality. Jump aboard – and fasten your seat belt!

Best

People often ask me, 'How can I be the best that I can be?' I tell them it's too late for that. Just try to be better than you are now. I didn't used to be and now I am. Better than I was. I had hardly any friends at school and now I have plenty of contacts in my database.

Big Ten

Like high-five but double (i.e. with both hands).

Binge Succeeding

What we all tend to do. We just think that if we focus on our goals really hard one day, we can take it easy the next. You get up early, you GIVE GOOD MEETING, you assert to flirt, you focus on GOALS, you believe to achieve. You ring up a not-so-warm contact out of the blue and grab a meet, you lead a light lunch which is totally targeted, you achieve breakthrough with a team trauma, you network big time at a semi-social occasion, you eat the right food, people ask your advice, you mentor here and facilitate there, you bring home the bacon, you seal a deal, you feel mighty real. But Luton Airport wasn't built in a day. Don't go overboard and then the next day slip back into the Sludge of Sameness. You may blow it. Keep on keepin' on. Don't let your Volcano of MOTIVITALITY spout it all out one day and lose all your Lava of LEADERSHIP.

Being a SUCCEEDER is about doing it full-time. Yesterday, today, tomorrow, the day after next week. Think five-a-day. Look into the mirror five times a day and say, 'You are a Succeeder' five times. And at weekends too. You can have bank holidays off.

Aim to Succeed at Least Five Times a Day!

Blame

The Blame Game is such an easy one to play. Have you ever uttered these words?

I knew it would never work.

This was your idea all along.

It was your fault I slept with that waitress.

In business and in life, we expend so much energy apportioning blame that we forget to move on, to find the solutions. We are too busy focusing on problems. Do these seem familiar?

Who can I blame for this?

I want to make sure everyone knows it was X's fault.

Maybe if you'd been more attentive I wouldn't have
    done what was basically waiting to happen.

So my advice is, seek first to blame yourself. What could you have done better? If that doesn't help, then think who else might have made a pig's ear of things and let them know.

See also ANGER.

Blood, Sweat & Tears (BST)

Vital in today's fast-moving business environment (FMBE). People think that sweat is just for certain occupations – plumbing, gym attendant, fire-fighter, etc. No, sir! Even if you're doing the whitest of white-collar jobs, there's no excuse for not giving it your all. I worked my way up. I shed blood, I sweated buckets and I wept a river of rage. It's only for that reason that now I don't need to work so hard. Maybe one day you could be like me, because no longer do I work hard. I work smart. In fact, I work smart casual, that's how smart I am.

However, there's no point giving BST in the wrong job. According to some projections by Professor Krench, 53 per cent of people are in the wrong job. Are you one of them? Stand back. Ask yourself some basic questions:

Is this really what I should be doing?

Should I really be banging my head against this brick wall? (Clue: NO!)

Is there something else I could be doing that is more like what I should really be doing?

So, if you haven't shed blood, sweat or tears today, then you know the day isn't over yet (unless it's a bank holiday).

Is there magic in your job? Time for some abracadabra! Hocus-pocus – time for change! What you need is focus. Without focus, you can't see through the lens of life. It's like magic!

Make Focus Your Pocus!

Hocus-focus – it's magic! Some people say success is 99 per cent perspiration and 1 per cent inspiration. There's more to it than that. There's also 66 per cent aspiration on top of those two!

Body Language

The subtle cues we give that tell people our true state of
mind. For example, use eye contact to your advantage.
People like it if you give them long glances, especially
members of the opposite sex. This is useful in negotiations
and networking opportunities but not mixed saunas or the
waiting room of relationship counsellors. With Mandy (ex-
dancer and graduate of many a SUCCEEDER weekend, who has
a wealth of showbiz experience, having been an extra on
TV's *Midsomer Murders*), I have created a Succeeder Body
Language course. Here is a simple guide:

Good for Business	Bad for Business
Smiling	Pouting
Shaking hands	Shaking head
Open aspect	Open flies
Waiting at a door	Pointing at the door
Jaw-jaw	Jab-jab
High-fiving and Big-tenning	Crying
Punching the air	Punching the host

Books

Lots of business books have been written – enough to cover
the world in forest thirty-eight times over – apparently.
Recent research by Professor Trankin of the Jimmy Connors
Institute tells us that only 17.4 per cent of them are actually
read, while 89 per cent of them are carried around in hand
luggage in the hope that their contents will migrate into the
businessperson's psyche while they're watching Argentinian
football in a hotel room at three in the morning.

Boot Camp

Every August I run a Business Boot Camp, a kind of 'Back to School' weekend for the recovering businessperson. We rise at 6 a.m., go for a run before BREAKFAST, which is eaten in silence while everyone reads the *Financial Times*.

Here's how the rest of the weekend pans out.

Saturday

07.00 Breakfast

07.30 Buzzness Basics I: Moisturiser

09.00 Movement and Dance, then Circle of Love

11.00 Break (in silence)

11.15 Case Study: 'How I Changed the Face of Refrigerated Transport' by L. Vaughan Spencer

13.00 Lunch (salad and pulses and song)

14.00 Personal Testimony: each participant tells his or her own story. L-Vo tells them where they have gone wrong

16.00 Break

16.30 Positive Thinking: What Have I Done Quite Well This Week?

18.00 Dinner

19.00 Create Moti-Mantra

20.00 Urban Tribal Drumming

21.00 Bedtime (read article on Business Bling by L. Vaughan Spencer from the *Dunstable Gazette*)

Sunday

06.30 Chanting of Moti-Mantra during Breakfast

07.15 Business Basics II: Clothes

09.00 Deep-Tissue Ego Massage with Cranston and his team of former paramilitaries

10.00   Break

10.15   Business Basics III: Know Thyself, Know Thy Elf

12.00   Movement and Dance

12.30   Lunch

13.15   Drawing the Future: Change Through Crayons.
        Critique by L-Vo

15.00   The Journey Ahead

15.30   Burst the Balloon of Failure

16.15   Discounted Cost Analysis

16.30   Going-Home Time (goody bags optional £12.50 with
        Succeeder CD, T-shirt and Succeeder Moisturiser)

The Boss

Bruce Springsteen, according to some. But he isn't really your boss – unless you are in the E Street Band, and even then only during touring and rehearsals. I imagine it's all done on a freelance basis.

Think of your boss. Is he nice? Or she (because ladies can be bosses too now)? What are your differences and similarities? What if you were his/her boss? This is called Managing Upwards. No, not managing on the stairs or in a lift but handling your superiors better. Could I be nicer to him? When was the last time I told her she was doing a good job? Can I buy him a present? Could I tell her how nice her hair is looking? Should I really be going to his/her boss every time something goes wrong in order to try to undermine him/her?

Is yours a Bonzer Boss?
Or a Bummer Boss?
Does he get cross?
Is he glum like Kate Moss?

Or is she full of fun like Jonathan Ross?
Does she bring kudos?
Or does he need some dental floss?

Boundary

Something for pushing (*see also* ENVELOPE).

Box

See THINKING OUTSIDE.
See also TICKING.

Boy Power

Like Girl Power (the post-post-feminist (PPF) theory first articulated by the Spice Girls. It's about it being all right again for women to be sporty, or scary, or posh or ginger. My friend Frederick tells me that actually it means that women can now feel empowered by wearing skimpy clothes), but for Men.

See also NEW VIRILITY.

Boy-sturiser

Moisturiser for the younger man.
See also MOISTURISER.

Brain

Something of someone else's to be picked. Unless the issue at hand has officially been classed a no-brainer. We all know about left- and right-brain activity – two sides of the NEURO BUREAU. But what if you are using neither – being neither logical *nor* creative? This is what many leaders demand of us: 'Don't bother me with details, forget the big picture, just get on with it.' Professor Krench of Succeeder Lab has characterised the kind of thinking that is neither left (L-Mode) nor right (R-Mode) as in-between (I-Mode). The in-between brain comes up with such questions as:

'Did I leave the gas on?'

'Would all my socks fit into the salad compartment in my fridge?'

'Whatever happened to Haysi Fantayzee (creators of the hit "John Wayne Is Big Leggy")?'

Natural 'I-Moders' are neither intuitive nor organised. They are ideally suited to occupations needing neither an empathetic nor a rational approach – cashiers at local authority parking permit offices, door-to-door frozen-fish sellers or staff at Royal Mail sorting offices (where you have to go and pick up post, take proof of ID and only-ring-the-bell-once, they can't find your package and when eventually then they do, it turns out to be something that a friend hasn't put a stamp on). These people are neither followers nor leaders; I call them NFNLs or *Lollers*. Most businesses have plenty of them and eventually slow to their pace. It's the old 80:20 rule – 80 per cent of the people do 20 per cent of the work.

The I-Brain is ubiquitous. Can we harness it for individual and corporate success? Most people go into I-Mode in meetings. Someone is giving a very interesting presentation on Discounted Cost Analysis or Next Year's Health and Safety Budget Projections, and you think, 'What if cheese wasn't called cheese but was called Arnold instead?' or 'How many vowels are there in the word karaoke?' or 'I want to stand up and shout "I'm an Atomic Kitten – MIAOW!" at the top of my voice.' Professor Krench has called this Brain Bifurcation

– you should be thinking about one thing but you can't help thinking about something else. Succeedership is about channelling all those seemingly unprofitable thoughts into a viable business model. Why *not* have a cheese called Arnold? It could do very well with a certain demographic (e.g. staff at Royal Mail sorting offices). Or create an online 'Check the Number of Vowels in a Word' service ('Vowel-ipedia') – or a sock compartment in the fridge (who hasn't hankered after chilled footwear)? And when I did once bellow, 'I'm an Atomic Kitten – MIAOW', it certainly gave that business a jolt – exactly what that funeral parlour needed. So the I-Brain can be made to work to your BUZZNESS advantage.

Train Your I-Brain!

Breakfast

The most important meal of the day. Do you know the saying, 'Breakfast like a king, lunch like a prince and dine like a whore in the kitchen'? Or something. But no businessperson can hope to make a contribution on a snatched piece of toast or, worse, just a cup of coffee. You need to get your energy up with some good carbs – porridge (which my American friends call oatmeal for some reason) or some barley and quinoa waffles or some Motivational Muffins. Take time to focus on the upcoming day. And why not join us for one of our Succeeder Breakfasts? We hold these regularly at the Ramada Jarvis Hotel, Watford. A couple of speakers come along and talk to us about a matter of great import. This month it was 'Managing Tricky Workplace Situations Involving People'. The speakers were L. Vaughan Spencer and ex-Luton Town footballer and part-time motivational speaker Les Goodhall. We touched on non-verbal and verbal communication skills, dealing with hurtful gossip and shirt-tugging in the penalty box. Next month, I've asked Frankie B to talk on 'Intellectual Property and Theft', but don't hold your breath.

Case Study

An executive was running out of puff at about 11 a.m. and gorging on chocolate and coffee. Succeeder Solutions made him have breakfast each day. Now he is nice until lunchtime, though often late for work.

Breathing

Vital in today's fast-moving business environment (FMBE). Without a doubt. Very important when presenting. And in most business situations. A business leader who isn't breathing isn't going to be effective, but sometimes people forget. Try a breathing exercise now.

Breathe in
Breathe out

Feels good, doesn't it? Keep going like that for the rest of the day. Useful at night-time, too.

Brotox

Like Botox – but for men. A last resort, mind! *See* MAKE YOUR FACE FIT© and MOISTURISER.

Budget

Make sure you spend it. All of it. If necessary, this may mean ordering about 4 million paperclips as your year-end approaches. Or multiple copies of this book. Remember, anything can be justified on the training budget – from lunch, to Wii games and tennis rackets.

Business

People ask me if I'm a life coach or a business coach. Let me tell you a secret. There is no difference. Business Is Life – Life Is Business!

Lose sight of that and you lose sight of *everything*. I talk about personal issues – self-esteem, clothes and moisturiser. These are vital in today's fast-moving business environment (FMBE). And conversely, if only you were more aware of business, your personal life would be better. For example, think of your friendships from a business point of view – is there sufficient return on investment? *See* FRIENDSHIP AUDIT.

Business Bling

Are you armed with Business Bling? People often ask me if it's OK for men to wear jewellery. Damn right it is! It's more than OK. Women understand the importance of power pearls, business brooches and empathetic earrings. Come on, guys! Get a SUCCEEDER signet ring and a no-nonsense necklace! Many men already wear a wedding ring. I don't any more. A 'nose-stud' could be just the thing to enhance your career. Accessorise to Motivitalise!

Business Express

The train that rushes along the tracks of commerce. Whoo-whoo – all aboard! Or have you missed the train? Did it leave the platform while you were in the Waiting Room of Life? Or maybe you were at the wrong station! If you did catch it, have you found your seat? Do you have a Saver Return or was it cheaper to get two singles? One day you can make it to First Class. But don't forget the Quiet Coach, where you can turn off your mobile and simply HOCUS-FOCUS on your destination. Let's hope you make the connection.

Businesspeople in Need

My favourite charity. I am a trustee. This is dedicated to helping those who have suffered while serving in the valiant cause of business. For example, we help those who have suffered flip-chart accidents, got their fingers caught in a filing cabinet, hyperventilated when presenting or taken a team-building exercise too far. We have a benevolent fund to which you can apply if you have failed to claim expenses within normal time limits, need a new suit for a job interview or have suffered the sudden and unexpected loss of a company car.

[*Ned*: You suggested putting their website here. I think it best not to distract the reader. Remember the motivational pound only goes so far and we want them to focus on Succeeder merchandise.]

Business Plan

An exciting story that gives everyone confidence in the future, like a fairy tale or *Neighbours* on the telly. Without one, there is no meaning in life. It impresses bank managers and investors. Without a map you cannot begin a journey. Any map will do, even if the map is of central Watford and you're in the Himalayas. For example, when I started the L. Vaughan Spencer Foundation, all I had was an idea. I didn't have a business plan. Maybe I had a riff but I hadn't written the song, let alone recorded the album, or prepared the artwork and story-boarded the promo video. I knew what I wanted – to make the world a better place. That's one heck of a business plan, and it ain't easy to cost it, but I knew we had to get an office. The very next day I rented one at the Spring Lakes Business Park. Then came Nikki. I played tennis with her dad. She slotted right in. She knew how to run an office. OK, she didn't share the vision – yet. But pretty soon, thanks to our daily morning SUCCEEDER WARM-UP and APPRECIATION HOUR, she found her HOCUS-FOCUS, and we could lay down the rhythm tracks. Pretty soon, I was working on the solos – being invited to the Luton Chamber of Commerce, uploading podcasts, giving out flyers at the Harlequin Shopping Centre in Watford. The SUCCEEDER SOUND was born. Maybe your business plan has facts and figures, but if you don't have a dream, all you'll have is BUSY-NESS.

See also BUZZNESS PLAN.

Business Process Re-engineering

Re-engineering a business process. Very, very important. Vital in today's fast-moving business environment (FMBE).

[*Ned*: Once we have our internet connection back and I can take a look at Wikipedia, this will be a rip-roaring entry. Liam has had a lot of soccer practice this week. I have increased his pay for next week and given his mother a piece of my mind.]

Busy-ness

That thing whereby you just do stuff all day and you don't know why. Too many people are in busy-ness, not business – running around taking calls, attending meetings, heading up never-gonna-happen project feasibility meetings, and mired in email maelstrom (*see* EMAILSTROM). Actually, I wouldn't mind having access to email once in a while. I haven't sent out this month's MOTIVITALITY e-missive (*Succeed-e-Zine*). There's an internet café near home which seems full of young French students so I've avoided it. But it might be worth just one trip in case my inbox is bulging.

Buzz

That ineffable feeling you can get from business. Can you feel the Buzz of Business right now? Look around. Is it coursing through your organisation? If not, get the buzz going. So how do you get the buzz going? You could try some URBAN TRIBAL DRUMMING or karaoke or get everyone to bring their pet to work. Alternatively, bring in a professional – a prize-fighter, a heavyweight. Some call me the Muhammad Ali of Motivation. Float like a butterfly, sting like a Myers-Briggs INTP! With me, you'll get to the weigh-in early and won't throw in the towel.

Buzzness

The buzz that is gained specifically from business. It's addictive. In fact, I often don't talk about business – only buzzness. As in

'I'm in the personal development buzzness.'
'Can I give you my buzzness card?'
'We have a great buzzness plan.'

Buzzness folk feel different. They smell different.

Are You in Buzzness?

Buzzness Bath

What you take at the end of a day in BUZZNESS. Wash away problems, soak up ideas with Succeederomatherapeutic bath gels (*see* Appendices).

Buzzness Card

An exciting icon of intent. But ask yourself this. Why should it be made of card? Why should it be rectangular? Here are some alternative shapes:

> Circular
> Cylindrical
> Cuboid
> Arrow (like those guitars in the 1970s)

Some alternative materials so that your card really makes an impression:

> Cheese
> Metal
> Tobacco
> Water
> Pâté de foie gras

Buzzness Plan

Something of poetic beauty. Different from a business plan in that it gets everyone buzzing. If a business plan is a burger and fries, a buzzness plan is a sirloin steak with sauté potatoes washed down with a top-notch Spanish sparkling wine. It could be a poem or it could be a story. It may not even have words – it could just be a drawing or a graph. Here is my personal buzzness plan:

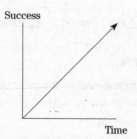

Can-Do

1. The attitude of someone who can do things. It's a state of mind. Some people think there is no such word as can't. There is. And cannot is a word, too. But don't use it.
2. Can-Do is also a new form of motivational martial art to replace Kendo. It's a halfway house to SUCCEE-DO, the motivational martial art.

Carbon Neutral

This is all about carbon dioxide and methane, which are emitted by buildings and cows and people – especially during MEETINGS. To make meetings carbon neutral, sometimes it's best not to talk at all. This way much more can get done. Don't waste paper by having an agenda or minutes. Just feel them. Let issues emerge organically.

I'm big into green. I love the green scene. I simply don't use plastic shopping bags. I bought one of those hessian ones for £5 from the local sandal-and-beard shop, though I do find it a bit itchy on my leg when I'm wearing shorts.

Be Seen to Be Green!

I'm glad to say that the clothes I'm wearing are made from sustainable forests, as is this book, Ned tells me. So the more you buy, the more forests will be planted, so you will be saving the world as well as yourself. Certainly, I've reduced my air miles lately. I would have no reason to go to Canada any more, even if there weren't some quite unjustified accusations hanging over me there. I get the train into London from Luton Parkway if I need to go there for business meetings, which is normally around mid-April. Driving to the office is necessary, though. There isn't a bus route to the Spring Lakes Business Park (well, there is, but it stops ten minutes' walk away). And Nikki was excellent at recycling paper. It's very important that you have a Sustainability Officer (or DEAN OF GREEN, as I call them).

Career

The world has changed. In the old days you would have a job for life. It was all straight clear lines. You knew where you were. Now, thanks to Stephen Hawking, time is curved, so we have a parabola of portfolio careers. What shape is your career? Don't think of it as a pole or a ladder with snakes in waiting; think of it as a windy garden path with weeds in the gaps. Or think of building a career as like creating a meal. In the past people had a starter, a main course and a pudding. Or they might have finished off with cheese and eventually some coffee and little biscuits. But nowadays people are much more into tapas – a portfolio of small career dishes. You dip into one and soon another comes along. You may still end up without much money and a bit hungry. Or is your career like a hotel buffet, where they give you a small kidney-shaped plate and you try to get as much as you can on it but the lettuce falls off the edge?

See also ENCORE CAREER, GAMING (STEER YOUR CAREER) and TRENDOLOGIST.

Case Studies

These are invaluable. You look at why a certain company went bust and try to work out why so that you don't do the same. Or why they were so successful. I have asked to be a case study for the Kall-Kwik School of Business at the University of the Isle of Wight. I'm hoping they'll pay enough for me to take on an office temp to get things like my internet connection sorted.

CEO

Chief Executive Officer. What I am of the L. Vaughan Spencer Foundation and the Succeeder Institute and Succeeder Solutions. If you're looking for the buck, you'll find it stopped right here! Ouch. If you want to be at the top, it's no good having altitude sickness. Or ATTITUDE SICKNESS.

Does your head honcho
Wear a poncho?
Does your big cheese
Know his elbow from his knees?
Does your CEO
Need some bravado?
You can't order leadership from Ocado!

Chalk 'n' Talk

The old way of training, learning and development. I embrace the new methods – methods for the 22ND CENTURY

– downloadable MP3 (Motivational Podcasts). And we are even looking at rolling out some training using Succeeder Scratch 'n' Sniff cards with prizes for the right answer. For example:

> One of the team you are leading asks for the afternoon off to attend their child's concert. Do you
>
> (a) Say no?
> (b) Say yes as long as they make it up another time
> (c) Take everyone along as a team-building exercise
>
> Now scratch off a, b or c. You can only scratch one.
> Can you smell success?

Change

Business today is all about change. If you're not changing you're the same as you were before and that's not the way to be. Are you scared of change?

Believe in Change – and Not Small Change!

Think of Doctor Who. He had the power to change. He was played by several different actors before becoming Scottish. He's got a big Tardis which looks small from the outside. Is that how your life looks? You've got to keep moving, changing, evolving, shedding skins like a snake. Or an onion.

Change Agent

A professional changer. There are some top Change Agents out there. They help roll out change. People think I am an Agent of Change. Oh no, I am much more. I am an Angel of Change. A recent award-winning change programme I effected won the Beds/Herts Bronze Lemur Award. You can read about it in the next issue of the fully peer-reviewed semi-quasi-academic journal *Success & Succeediness*.

Change Champion

Someone who is really excited about a forthcoming Change Programme. Find them, nurture them. Proclaim them your CSO (Chief Succeedy Officer)! They are your WARRIORS, your agents provocateurs, the yeast in your bread of banality. History wouldn't have been the same if there hadn't been Change Champions championing change. Think of all the areas where there's been a paradigm shift. For example, we'd still be using abacuses if it weren't for Señor Casio or eating badly if it hadn't been for Delia. Here are some examples of people who revolutionised the way we see things:

Radio	Tennis
Alexander Graham Bell [*Ned*: or was he the telephone?]	Virginia Wade
	Anna Kournikova
Jimmy Saville	Tim Henman
Steve Wright in the Afternoon	

France	Air Travel
Louis XIV	The Wright Bros.
Napoleon	Richard Branson
Thierry Va-Va-Voom Henry	The person who invented very small packets of peanuts

Hotels	Science
Paris Hilton	Albert Einstein
Mr Ramada	Maggie Philbin
Mr Jarvis	Patrick Moore

Television	Cooking
John Logie Baird	Delia Smith
Sue Barker	Jamie Oliver
Neighbours	The chef at La Grande Bouche, Harpenden

Cars	Business
Henry Ford	Adam Smith
Knight Rider (with David Hasselhoff)	Evan Davis
	L. Vaughan Spencer
Richard Hammond	

Chapitalism

Old-style, male-dominated 'gentlemanly' business. In England, it was all about the 'Old Boy Network'.

See also LIPSTICK LEADERSHIP *and* CHICK-ITALISM.

Cheese & Business

Cheese is the perfect metaphor for business. That's why I, and so many others, have written at length about it and why I sit on the European Cheese Council. Here are some basic lessons:

☆ Don't over-milk a cash-cow.

☆ As with business skills, there are both hard and soft cheeses. And if the soft stuff goes off, things get very smelly indeed.

☆ Storage can be an issue.

Certainly, cheese gives us a great dairy metaphor for LEAD-ERSHIP. Each of your team members can be thought of as a goat, a sheep or a cow. The goat can climb to great heights and forage for food, the sheep follows the herd but keeps them together, and the cow sits down when it's about to rain. And what of your leadership style if it were a cheese? Is it hard or soft? Or does it have a rough rind and a softness inside? Or does it just stink to high heaven?

Chick-italism

Capitalism for Chicks. The new post-Chapitalist approach to BUSINESS – more about CSR, sustainability and holding hands. It's more female-friendly and fashion-aware. Just think if the originator of capitalism were not *Adam* (Smith) but *Eva* (Longoria – of *Desperate Housewives*).

Children

Our future – *without a doubt*. Who will be the leaders of tomorrow? Probably the same ones as today unless they're sacked overnight, but who will be our leaders in twenty years' time? Children – well, people who are children now. Who will be the leaders in forty years' time? Today's slightly younger children, or people who haven't been born yet, but who will be children before they become leaders. And who are the most creative individuals in the world? 'I believe that children are our future,' sang Whitney Houston, and I won't disagree. Of course, business can learn from children. Isn't it great when they can come in on Bring Your Children to Work Day? They can do some menial work and fetch coffee, sandwiches, etc. Or often they can ask questions that go right to the heart of the business. Here are some I've overheard:

Why is that man shouting so much?
Why doesn't anyone clean up these coffee cups?
Why isn't anyone talking to anyone else?
Who's in charge?

What does this company actually do?

Don't you think this place should introduce Six Sigma methodology?

Here is a transcript of a talk I gave at Skybrook Primary School Careers Evening recently:

Hello, boys and girls, mummies and daddies and teachers. My name is L. Vaughan Spencer, but you can call me L-Vo. I'm a business and self-help guru. If you haven't heard the word guru before, don't worry. It just means teacher – a really, really good teacher.

Do you know what you're going to do when you grow up? Anybody want to be a fire-fighter? I thought so! Anybody want to be an astronaut? Anybody want to be on telly? Most of you. Great. But I want you to think about something else – business or Buzzness, as I call it. It's as exciting as anything! It's just as great as Ant & Dec and an iPod! You have to put out metaphorical fires, you will go into uncharted space – and you may end up on telly! Isn't that great! You get to work on a computer, go to meetings and maybe even drive a car! And you might end up with a pension as well – though nowadays it's unlikely to be based on your final salary.

Chill Day

When you take things easy, as opposed to a STRESS Day or a DONKEY DAY. Chant, divest yourself of old habits (or clothes) or collect your receipts and put them in an envelope.

See SUCC-STRESS.

Chromatic Intelligence

Like EMOTIONAL INTELLIGENCE (EQ) but this is understanding about colours.

See also COLOUR THERAPY.

Circle of Trust

Your inner circle; your mini-mentors; those who would die for you. I haven't asked anyone to do this for me yet. I know my friend Charles would. After all, he gave up his job, house and family (and car) to help fund the cause of Success. I'm not sure my good friend Les Goodhall (ex-Luton Town FC) would go this far. He didn't manage to make it to the Careers Evening I organised at Skybrook Primary School. 'Diary clash,' he said. So it was left to me to talk to the older children about coaching, consulting and all the really exciting things of BUZZNESS. I didn't want to go too far too quickly, so we left Structured Investment Vehicles till next term.

Circus

A great metaphor for business. There are clowns as well as ELEPHANTS in the room. You have to keep the animals separate, throw them scraps of meat to do tricks, then muck out after them. The ringmaster gets the best costume but has no apparent skill himself. When I lived in Canada briefly, I used to visit lots of circuses. There were no animals, just pure human skill. My favourites were Le Cirque du Cyril, Cirque du Soulier and the Cirque du Merde, run by a man called Monsieur Merde. He would be a great speaker at one of our Succeeder Breakfasts.

Clothes

Vital in today's fast-moving business environment (FMBE). Professor Trankin found that 97 per cent of people wore clothes while conducting business.

What's the first thing people see when they meet you – after your face and your BUZZNESS CARD? Your clothes! So they really are important. Take a moment right now. Stop reading this book. Actually, read the two sentences after this one and the three after that, then stop, then come back quite soon after that. Look at your clothes. Are they saying the following?

Help! I need love.
I don't know who I am.
I just don't care.

I thought so. OK, time to start reading the book again now. Maybe I didn't need to write that sentence, because, if you read it, you are already back reading the book. But you take my point.

So what are the clothing howlers that won't help you in BUZZNESS? Here are a few:

Novelty tie
Grass skirt
Beret (unless you are French)
Jumpsuit
Hoops (unless you are French)
Anything edible
Boob tube (unless you are French) or ruff

You can learn more through my audio Motivitalising Modules:

Dress 4 Success – Are Your Pants Holding You Back?
Are you Winter, Summer or Spring or Autumn?
You and Your Underpants – Are you prepared to say
    Goodbye?
How to Avoid Dressing Like a Caretaker

Business is based on relationships and impact. Without clothes, you've got no chance! Your business will suffer (apart from some particular businesses, obviously). So I offer in-depth Succeedy Sartorial Sessions. Please send photo.

Does Your Shirt or Skirt Help You Assert?

And isn't it time you had a COLOUR THERAPY consultation to enhance your CHROMATIC INTELLIGENCE?

Coach

Someone without whom life is impossible. Without a doubt. Do you have a coach? No? Ouch! Time to get one – a Results Coach, a Skills Coach, an Executive Coach, an Image Coach and, when you're ready, a Turbo Coach! For a small weekly outlay, you will see your career go into hypo-hyper-drive. Therapy deals with your past. Coaching creates your future, and can be done down the phone.

If you would like a coach, contact us at Succeeder Solutions. If you're lucky, you might even get me (at a premium, of course). At the moment, I have gaps on a Tuesday morning, Thursday afternoon and Friday, but I like to keep that as a CHILL DAY. For you, though, I might be willing to make an exception. Please send photo.

Tip-Top Coaching Tips for the BPD Professional Who Wants to Coach

Listen.

Repeat.

Nod (or say 'Mmm' if it's a phone session: *see* PHONIVATION©).

Coach Couch(es)

A couch for a coach to sit or lie on while coaching. I recommend LUTON FUTON.

¡CoachStock!

Every year in Davos, Switzerland, the World Economic Forum is held. It attracts the top leaders in business and politics. My brother, Nigel Spencer, MP for Luton (Airport South), is hoping to go next year – as the guest of a company that wants to build a combined nuclear power plant and bail hostel in his constituency in downtown Luton. In the same week, the Global Personal Development Forum (aka ¡Coach-Stock!) is held in Daventry. The world's top coaches and their wives (and husbands) gather to share advances and discoveries, and, let's be frank (but not Frankie!), show off a bit. If you are really interested in being a CHANGE AGENT in your company then you must attend. Through the L. Vaughan Spencer Foundation, you can get three tickets for the price of one. All you have to do is wear our branded leisure gear for the duration. Then go back to your company as CCC (Chief Change Commando) or CSO (Chief Succeedy Officer).

There is a Coach-Off, where a particularly difficult client is given five minutes with different coaches and the one who manages to get him or her to fully address their issues wins a bottle of sparkling wine. There are all sorts of stalls – for example, one promoting the latest coaching technology. Going beyond phone-coaching, there is now cyber-coaching, where for the right fee you can have a 3-D representation of your coach without him or her even having to listen to you. You can see the latest in COACH COUCHES, because, let's face it, who wants to help with other people's challenges in anything other than the most comfortable surroundings?

There are morning meetings at which we share the latest coaching models in sessions called 'Hey, Buddy, Can You Spare a Paradigm?' In the evenings, we let our hair down a bit. One year, I got together a scratch band of fellow personal development specialists. Despite our different disciplines, we muddled along somehow. We called ourselves the Coach Potatoes (Executive Coach Relief was an option we went with for a couple of days). We had a life coach, a nutritionist and a psychoanalyst (who had been in a Freudian tribute band called The Not So Happy Mondays). We couldn't stop arguing. Sadly, for musical reasons, it was decided that I shouldn't sing but just dance, a bit like Bez in the Happy Mondays. We did some covers (e.g. 'Voulez-vous Coacher avec Moi', 'S-S-S-Succeedio' by Phil Collins and Gloria Gaynor's 'I Will Succeed'). Despite the others not joining in my rigorous physical and vocal warm-up routine, I thought we did well but the others aren't interested in re-forming, even for a charity gig at Skybrook Primary School, where I know we can get the hall for free (plus maybe a bottle of sparkling wine for Mr Henderson, the caretaker!).

Colour Therapy

Do the colours you wear resonate with your personality? Or are you chromatically challenged? Are you wearing red when you should be wearing burgundy? Black when you should be in vermilion? Cerise when you should be in brown? Colour can affect your health, inner one-ness and bank balance. Colour is light. Colour is energy. Colour me bad – or colour me good!

Red is about sex and sales – which are very much in the same ballpark. It is the colour of fire and postboxes. But don't wear it when you are poorly or meeting someone in New Media.

Orange is the colour of wisdom and joy and finance. That's why I wear it a lot. Think of it as a weekend treat. Luton Town FC used to wear orange as their away kit.

Yellow is all about the solar plexus and LEADERSHIP. Good to wear on training days and with the in-laws. Can show the dirt, though.

Green has a calming effect and balances the nervous system, so wear it for appraisals. Green stimulates growth, so don't wear it if you're fat. Can work well on traffic wardens.

Blue is about the throat. Wear it for presentations, job interviews and a hot date when you're confident of a result. Could be good in a tie or a neck-scarf.

Indigo is the colour of intuition and IT. Don't wear it in budget meetings but do wear it on a first date. Unless it's with an insolvency practitioner.

Violet is the colour of project management so can give you a headache if incorrectly worn. Probably best in socks.

For more in-depth advice, get yourself along to someone who understands hues (like yours truly!). Take a look at my pic on the cover of this book. Yes, I am wearing autumn colours (or fall colors, as my American readers would have it). Autumn is a time of change, of renewal, of letting go. My leaves are dropping, so I'm ready getting to bud in the spring. I'm letting go of the past and looking forward to new adventures. Remember, the fall comes before pride. And I'm gonna be full of pride – when my leaves have come back.

Comfort Zone

Somewhere to get out of. Book your train ticket outta there right now – and don't buy a return, even if it's cheaper than a single which sometimes happens. Athletes talk about being 'in the zone'. They don't mean being in the Comfort Zone. They are in the Zone of Peak Performance. Well, in BUZZNESS we have to be in the Zone of Zest – a zest for life, a zest for business, which is the same thing.

> *It's always best in the zone of zest.*
> *Don't be in the zone of moan.*
> *It's time to own your zone!*

If you don't feel zest for your job, it's time to make tracks. Get out of town! Hop on board the BUSINESS EXPRESS!

Complexity

Business is complex. Most organisations are a series of competing wants, rivalries and silos. This is my Big Bang Theory of Businesses: they tend to have a Not Particularly Intelligent Design. But don't go trying to oversimplify things. You can't change an organisation simply by waving a magic wand. Unless you are a fairy godmother. Or a member of the Magic Circle. And even then you have to make sure you waved your wand in the right way. And that it was the right wand. Before I begin the process of completely overhauling an organisation, I make damn sure I understand it. I talk to the chief exec and, in the afternoon, I talk to the cleaners.

Compliments Book

All part of P-THINK (Positive Thinking Plus): instead of a suggestions book, you have a Compliments Book, where you can write nice things about fellow employees. I did this here at Succeeder Solutions. Here are some of the things in the book:

Your hair looks nice.

You smiled when you greeted me today.

It's really great when you make me a cup of coffee first
thing in the morning.

It seems I was the only one writing things in it – all the above are about Nikki. I keep leaving it lying around for Liam to add something about his sympathetic employer but he says he wants to try out some ideas for increasing Succeeder Solutions' income stream.

Conference Calls (Conf-Calls)

Vital in today's fast-moving business environment (FMBE) and essential when preparing an intervention. Your client(s) may be very busy or may not want to talk to you (I find this a lot). So gather round a table and you can really chew the cud remotely. A conference call is the oil in the Carburettor of Success. Many a BUZZNESS simply couldn't survive without what I call the Conf-Call. But there is a certain etiquette. So here are the answers to some FAQs:

Who does most of the talking?
The one with the deepest voice.

What do you do with your hands?
*Put them clearly on the table. Do not open noisy sweet
    wrappers, unless your call is about sweets.*

What do you say to introduce yourself?
Name, colour of clothing, and which animal you are.

Conferences

Vital in today's fast-moving business environment (FMBE). As we approach the 22ND CENTURY we are in the epoch of what I call Conference Capitalism. Today's Cathedral of Commerce is the well-equipped hotel with wi-fi, sauna and seminar room with felt-tip pens, flip charts and green boiled sweets. But conferences should not be taken lightly. Don't just arrange one because you had one last year and you've got a team whose sole function is to organise conferences. You must get a theme, a really clever one like these I have used below:

Building on Last Year's Successes

Teams can be subdivided into Bricks, Mortar, Plumbers and Plasterers for the breakout sessions and Let's Make a Video Competition.

Trees: Let's Put Down Roots for the Next Five Years

'OK, the Dutch elms can go to Seminar Room Seven and let's see what acorns you can come up with!'

Pop Stars: Next Year We Will Be Number One in the Hit Parade

(From the CEO's speech) 'What this company needs is a Whole Lotta Love, and Baby, I'm Your Man. Everything I Do, I Do It for You. Every Move You Make, Every Breath You Take, I'll Be Watching You. Don't You Wish Your Girlfriend Was Hot Like Me?'

Tinned Fruit

'And the winners of this year's karaoke were the Pineapples!'

Of course, follow-up is vital. Has everyone handed in their feedback form? Did they in the ensuing months wear their 'The Man from Supply Chain Logistics – He Say Yes! Conference 2003' branded socks? Did they start every meeting with the conference closing song, 'Can't Live If Livin' Is Without You' by Harry Nilsson and Mariah Carey?

Conflict Resolution

Resolving conflict. This is very important. I have learned a lot about this from my work with business and people and businesspeople. So I am putting something back into the community. I have established the L. Vaughan Spencer International Conflict Resolution Center. We meet once a month at the St Albans Community Association. I have let the United Nations know but it seems they are so interested in solving global conflict that they don't even bother replying to letters from leading motivators, even though somehow Frankie B gets invited to talk to a UNESCO coffee morning.

We offer our resolution service pro bono. That means for free. One teenage 'hoodie' thought he might get to meet U2. Anyway, he was grateful we sorted out his issue with the next-door neighbour over their barbecue, even if it did take a couple of months.

Have you encountered conflict that needs resolving? Business has plenty to learn from those Con-Res folk. Here are some Tip-Top Tips:

1. Let everyone feel they are part of the process.

2. Don't go in with any agenda. Literally. It's good to talk about what you're going to talk about before you talk about it, so everyone has chance to talk before actually talking.

3. Make sure everyone gets a chance to talk ('What about you, Philip? You've been awfully quiet. How do you feel about the genocide in your country?').

5. If someone seems to be doing all the talking, gently remind them that there are other voices to be heard ('That's all very well, Sean, but maybe you need to go on one of my Anger Management Modules').

6. Focus on achievable GOALS (e.g. where to have the coffee machine, whether to have *Steve Wright in the Afternoon* in the background).

*Consumer**

Consumers are supposed to buy things but they often don't behave as expected. That's why it's so important to do consumer research, something we do constantly at the L. Vaughan Spencer Foundation, asking things like:

Why did you choose this course?

How did you find out about it?

Did it meet your objectives?

Would you recommend it to a friend?

Did you prefer the shouting or the juggling?

Did you enjoy it (a) a lot (b) loads (c) it was like totally amazing!

As soon as Nikki is back we're going to collate everything

---

*You are a consumer of this book. Why not give us your feedback in the Appendices? You may win your company the chance of a consulting session from yours truly! Please send photo.

so I can move all those boxes of feedback forms from the kitchen.

Corporate Governance

Making sure that your free trips to the cricket/football/table-tennis or dinners/fashion shows/dungeon parties are seen as entirely necessary for the BUZZNESS. At a deeper level, says my friend Frederick, it's about making sure you're careful of that fine line between good business practice and homicide.

Cost-Cutting

In every business there will be bad times. But don't cut back on the one thing that will make your business a BUZZNESS: TRAINING.

Outside It May Be Raining
But Inside, We Carry on Training!

Success depends on training. The more training, the more success. It's obvious. Look at this graph.

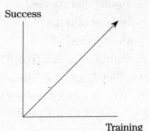

Creativising

Being creative either as a team or as an individual. I do a lot of one-man creativising on the futon in my office, with my eyes shut, while listening to *Steve Wright in the Afternoon.*

Cross-Reference

See CROSS-REFERENCE.

CSR

Corporate Social Responsibility. Vital in today's fast-moving business environment (FMBE). Every organisation must know what effect it is having on society. It should have a DEAN OF GREEN and know that it's not just about making a fat profit. That's why I am a governor of Skybrook Primary School. The Deputy Headmistress may be an absolute delight, but I'm there for the kids. And I think she's in a relationship anyway.

Culture (Corporate)

I was interviewed on this oh-so hot topic for Terminal Radio, the in-house broadcaster at London Luton Airport, by Robert Delano, who has since gone on to great things at Radio X-Pat FM in Marbella. So here is the transcript of the interview. I think it speaks for itself:

RD: L. Vaughan Spencer is the foremost commentator on corporate culture in the Luton/Watford/Stevenage area –

L-Vo: The Succeeder Triangle, as I call it.

RD: He has changed literally lots of organisations, and some of them had actually asked him to.

L-Vo: Without change, there can be no continuity. With the lightning pace of change in the internet world, if today you're still where you were yesterday, then tomorrow you won't be there any more. And someone else will tread on your toes. Having cold feet could be your Achilles heel.

RD: Quite. For you, what is corporate culture?

L-Vo: Good question, Rob. The dictionary will tell you that culture is 'a set of bacteria' like in a yogurt. So, business listener, is your company like a yogurt? Is it past its sell-by date? Has it gone a bit sour? Or is it low-fat with fruit and really yummy? Or one of those ones with one compartment for jam and one for the yogurt and you mix them up? Corporate culture is the thing that makes an organisation what it is and what it isn't. Without a corporate culture no organisation can survive … It's like a lion without a mane, a cappuccino without the froth, or Destiny's Child without Beyoncé. Booty-not-so-licious!

RD: Is this a Mission Statement that you're talking about?

L-Vo: No way, José! For example, a company's values may be subtle and unspoken:

1. Make as much money as possible.
2. In as little time as possible.

Whereas it may have a public Mission Statement that's been drafted by too many people and goes on and on about empowerment and being nice to children and animals. File it under F for Fiction!

RD: Why are we interested in a company's culture?

L-Vo: It's very important. Far too many organisations spend too much time trying to make things or sell them, instead of focusing on important things like corporate culture, or traffic-calming measures in the car park, or team-building events in hotels with trouser presses near motorways. This is the bread and butter of corporate culture. And without the bread and butter – where would you put your jam? (Possibly in your yogurt, but you take my point.)

RD: Does anyone really believe any of this anyway?

L-Vo: Most definitely. When I enter an organisation, I can almost smell the culture. Sometimes it smells of fear. Or fish. Sometimes fearful fish. Those who really know about corporate culture are outsiders like me. We don't work in the organisation, which means we can be objective and use words like 'paradigm' easily and tell them what to do and let them sort it all out when we've gone.

RD: So there we have it – corporate culture? L-Vo, thank you.

L-Vo: Thank you. Is there a car booked for me?

RD: No, but I can give you a lift home if you like.

L-Vo: Thanks.

RD: If you don't mind waiting till the end of the show in an hour and half.

L-Vo: OK.

RD: Now our next guest – the woman who lost her car in the multi-storey at the Harlequin Shopping Centre in Watford.

Customer Service

Vital in today's fast-moving business environment (FMBE). But what do you do if the customer is really cheesed off? Send your staff on our top course: 'The Totally Angry Customer'. Modules include:

☆ Calmness Through Breathing and Silent Ankle Exercises

☆ A 'Negative No' versus a 'Succeeder No'
☆ How to Empathise with Idiots
☆ How to Transfer the Call

CV (curriculum vitae)

(US) *Résumé*

The list of your achievements. In many ways it doesn't really say much. My CV may not be that impressive and the University of the Isle of Wight may not be up there with Harvard and Oxbridge, but my story is so much more complex. When writing your CV emphasise the positive. Here are some suggestions for giving a more complete picture:

Mundane	Buzzness
Worked in pub	Hospitality management
Worked in Primark	Retail management
Ran student disco	Event management
Holiday in Ibiza	Ran project in developing world
In Brownies or Cubs	Duke of Edinburgh Award Scheme
'Sixer' in Brownies or Cubs	Leadership position in youth movement
Acted in school play	Profound personal development work
Baby-sitting	Psychology internship
Attended salsa class	Culturally aware
Easily bored	Results-oriented
Collected jokes for student rag-mag	Journalism
Sacked for fiddling expenses	'The company's ambition didn't match mine'
Unemployed	Career break

Dadvertising

Advertising using portrayal of dads. No longer are they the strong, authoritative figures of our patriarchal past. Now they are bumbling, insensitive, ignorant oafs who notice nothing, can't make or mend anything and are lazy. OK, it's probably true, but this continual depiction means that men have forgotten that they were born to be WARRIORS – hunting their prey and attracting women, then defending them from wolves and bears and other men. The prey may now be business-focused achievable targets within set time frameworks, and the women may now be the boss setting the agenda, but men still need to understand their MANLINESS. So I have started the NEW VIRILITY movement. If you want to be Fully Virile and Fully New, then come on our Watford Warrior Weekend (refreshments and spear included).

Dance

Just like primitive people do the War Dance to prepare for war or the Rain Dance to create rain, the SUCCEEDER does the Succeeder Dance to engender HOCUS-FOCUS in heightened interfaces (job interview, presentation, first date, etc.). Using movements taken from whirling dervishes, salsa and some that Mandy made up, building on your P-MOVE, the Succeeder achieves One-ness, finding inner rhythm and even achieving altered or primal states on a good day. Ecstatic dance can water your soul in the Wilderness of Woe. Why not come on our Succeeder Dance Course? Wear loose clothing and bring your own packed lunch and plimsolls.

Data Decay

Whereby you lose people's addresses. Succeeder Solutions can assist in upholding your Data Integrity. Give us the names and addresses of your customers, suppliers and employees and we will make sure that they are used.

Dean of Green

Sustainability Officer. Every company should have one, making sure that you don't use plastic bags, that you recycle and turn off lights and that you have a hybrid car. I see myself as the Al Gore of business (though of course I've yet to win an Oscar® for a documentary about my work. But it's in hand ... I'm working with one of the dads from Skybrook on a fly-on-the-wall film called *The Luton Leader*). Obviously, if being green compromises your business, best not to bother.

Decision-Making

Vital in today's fast-moving business environment (FMBE). Many leaders do little else other than decision-making. 'Don't give me sense – give me a decision!' is the oft-heard refrain in many companies today. Think of Decide as De-Side. You're on nobody's side. You consider everyone's Upside and Downside before your De-Side, though it's hard not to get Off-Side.

Difference (aka Diff)

1. Something that I try to make. Wherever I go, I make damn sure that things are different when I leave – whether it be a company, a coachee's life or an elevator full of people. My interventions have made such a difference that many clients haven't needed me to come back.

2. Standing out from the crowd. I make a difference by being different. Nobody wears clothes or talks like I do. Difference is good.

   See also DUDE OF DIFF.

Difficult People

Let's face it, every organisation has them … control freaks, whingers, show-offs, gossips, know-alls and 'oh-no-it'll-never-workers'. I call them the IRRITATI. These 'dark side' tendencies erode productivity and retention and can lead to LEADERSHIP Derail. At Succeeder Solutions we try to deal with them at the recruitment stage or when a client tells us a colleague is getting on their nerves. Dysfunctional behaviours surface when people are

☆ Lacking Chill Time
☆ A bit tired
☆ Eating the wrong things
☆ Wearing non-harmonious colours
☆ Failing to moisturise
☆ Needing a cuddle
☆ Getting a lot of hassle from the Other Half
☆ Irritating

How does the SUCCEEDER deal with them? This is one of

the things I learned from observing the primitive AYCH-ARE tribe. They generally sit such people down in the forest and tell stories of situations analogous to where the Irritato has been getting on people's wick. They just don't tell them about tribal meetings, or move their tent when they're off hunting. If these fail, they start 'bigging them up' to other tribes in the hope that the other tribe will want them and then they get transferred.

I use various methods, either carrot or stick (metaphorically, but feel free to try it literally too):

☆ Ignore them
☆ Cuddle them
☆ Promote them
☆ Make them cry
☆ Write a letter to their mum
☆ Send a drawing of them anonymously to TV's *Crimewatch*.

Digital Footprint

The information that is available on the internet about each of us. Of course, nowadays much of that has been placed by ourselves. But beware: putting a funny photo of yourself in fancy dress on MySpace or Facebook and tagging it 'What a Tart!' could spoil your chances of getting that job in financial services or at a nursing home. What you should do is upload pictures of yourself being Succeedy or in a leadership position or giving a top presentation on strategy parameters to leading members of the buzzness community. Prospective employers and academic institutions do check these things out.

[*Ned*: – I checked your Facebook page. Shouldn't a pirate wear more than a hat and a bottle of strategically placed champagne?]

Why not check out my MySpace and Facebook pages and say hi?

Diversity

How does a company treat people who aren't normal (white, middle class and male, like me)? For example, how does it look after the ladies? Are there pretty flowers in the lobby for them to look at and nice smellies in the bathroom? Is there a glass ceiling? Because this could make it very cold in the winter and you know how girls feel the cold. Here are some more Motivational Podcasts to help you become a champion for Diversity:

Things We Can Learn from the Ladies

Not All Lesbians Wear Dungarees

Ethics – Trying to Avoid Favouring the Pretty Girl

Doin' the Deal

There is no satisfaction like Doin' the Deal. Here are some examples: -

Yes, I agree to publish your book.

Yes, we will pay you a hundred and twenty quid to be the lead speaker at our car dealers' convention.

OK, I will give you my phone number.

These are music to my ears. The deal is done, both parties are satisfied and a successful commercial relationship is cemented. A BUZZNESS deal which is pure WIN/WIN/WIN is a thing of beauty – like an egg and cress sandwich washed down with sparkling wine on a summer's evening overlooking Mid-Herts Golf Course.

'Doing a deal makes you feel like you are immortal. Thanks L-Vo! I am invincible!'

Duncan Cherry, Luton Fridge Shelf Replacements

'L-Vo taught me the importance of closing a deal.'

Timothy, Spiritual Alchemy Associates

Dolphins in Business

People are always going on about how dolphins are highly intelligent, so how come not a single one has been asked to lead a FTSE 100 company? I think the case is overstated. But they are terribly relaxing and I've seen them clean their own teeth with a huge brush at aqua-parks. Have you ever swum with the dolphins? I swam with the dolphins in Torquay. Dolphins are the Angels of the Sea. I think of myself as a dolphin – when I'm not thinking of myself as a lion.

Male dolphins organise themselves into three tiers of friends and accomplices, roughly translated as:

I'd Help Him Move House

I'd Lend Him a Fiver

All Right to Go for a Drink with

This calibration could be useful in your FRIENDSHIP AUDIT. The dolphins do this through elaborately synchronised twists, leaps and spins – much the same as a group of young men on a Friday or stag night, though they achieve harmony through grunts, laughter and funny photos on their mobile phones.

When I am not aligned or have stress management issues I just go back to that place in my mind – I go to my mental

THE EMOJI MOVIE

n, but Kiefer as a place. The
n he is applying layer upon
raw and ash to a canvas. A
ward the end of the war and
early 75 years now. A place
istory, religion, literature,
s are brought together, and
sees is infinite, because it is
everyone who sees it. It is a
een the river and the forest.
aclitus said and wrote about
s immutable and always the
ote in response, and Heide-
r of the forest, let his philos-

Torquay – and I swim with them. I want you to come with me to Torquay, reader … Are you free? Come with me right now … Sit back and imagine swimming. You are swimming with the dolphins … Swim, swim, swim, swim. Do you feel relaxed? I bet you do! From now on, when you need to relax, focus on Swim/Swim. This is Dolphin-Focused Visualisation (DFV).

Swim/Swim = Win/Win

Would you like to come on a Dolphin Experience? Many people have benefited from this, especially those in the public sector. Obviously, it can be a bit pricey getting to the coast or flying to Tenerife, so we do our own version at the Watford Ramada Jarvis with a couple of inflatables. But we don't have to worry about wind and weather and drowning. We also do dolphin-style meditation classes.

Donkey Day(s)

A day for doing Donkey Work – moving boxes, paying gas bills, seeing marriage guidance counsellors. As opposed to CHILL DAYS or WOW DAYS.

Downside

The bad things that will happen as a result of something. *See also* UPSIDE. Sometimes there's a downside to the upside. That's upside-downside.

Dragon

Something that lives in a den and may give money to would-be entrepreneurs on telly. (There's also the Dragon of Failure – *see* HAIR). I did write and apply to be one of the Dragons when the sushi guy left but then realized you had to use your own money. Typical corner-cutting by these TV types.

See also TELEVISION.

Dress-Down Friday

Part of the so-called WAR ON TALENT, later misinterpreted by George Bush. To keep your talented young people, you allow them to come to work in casual clothes on a Friday because it's nearly the weekend. If I do go into the office, I wear my tracksuit, which makes daily WARM-UP more comfortable. Nikki doesn't seem to get the idea and insists on wearing a trouser suit come what may. Liam, on the other hand, seems to think that every day is a Dress-Down Day. His jeans barely cover his underpants and the crotch is somewhere near the knees. But he has managed to secure sponsorship for some of our motivational podcasts, so he must be doing something right.

This is a difficult area. Remember, though, that 'business casual' still puts the biz first. Avoid yoga pants (unless it's a MEET-ERCISE) and golf shirts. Don't wear sandals. Here's a rough rule of thumb: the more body parts you show, the less personal power you have. Respect given is inversely proportional to amount of skin showing. Look at this graph:

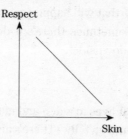

Make sure you are ready for BUZZNESS, not the beach.

Dude of Diff

There Is Nobody Like Me
We Are All Unique!

Can the same be said of you? Be different. Be your own USP.
Read different newspapers, have different hair, walk different corridors, though beware of fire exits. Once I got stuck
in a stairwell going nowhere. I couldn't call anyone on my
mobile as there was no coverage. I got panicky and opened
a fire door, thus setting off an alarm. I had to return my entire
coaching fee to reimburse the company for the inconven-
ience caused, plus send a signed photo to the fire brigade.

> *What's the Diff?*
> *Are you ready to jump off the cliff?*
> *Yeah, that's the Big If.*
> *What's the Diff?*
> *Are you a legend or a myth?*
> *You don't need to be bored stiff.*
> *Maybe it's time to sport a quiff!*
> *And rock your rebranding riff!*

Edge

1. As in *cutting, leading, even bleeding*, often *lacking in*. What every organisation needs or needs to be on. L-Vo likes to be on the edge – because from the edge you get a better view of the centre.

   See also EDGY.

2. The guitarist of U2. The one with the hat. And the guitar.

Edgy

When there's just too much EDGE. Edgy means you've edged too near the edge and fallen off.

Education

People talk about going to the School of Hard Knocks or the University of Life. Huh! I did a postgrad diploma in 'Rolling with the Punches: What Doesn't Kill You Makes You Stronger and the Devil Take the Hindmost'! Let's just say my dissertation was measured not in words but in BLOOD, SWEAT AND TEARS. There were bad times, yet somehow only when you're in the gutter can you really see where the pavement ends. So, only three years after having just 19p to my name, I had created a business with a turnover in excess of £12,000. How did I do it? I knuckled down and within a week I had written a book on how to be successful, called *Overnight Success within a Week*. And it's still in print in seventy-four languages, with the interactive video game available soon. When the chips are down, who you gonna call? Ghostbusters? I don't think so! The only person you can rely on is yourself – not your ELF. Nobody else can do your homework. Life is continuous assessment. It's a big lesson but one that I learned in the Kindergarten of Nice Guys Finish Last!

E-Learning

Learning through E – electronically. Nothing to do with going to a rave. As well as Scratch 'n' Sniff, we are developing many innovative ways for up-to-the-minute training:

> M-Learning – on your mobile
> T-Learning – in the toilet
> S-Learning – slow learning for dimbos
> X-Learning – adults only

See also LEARNING.

Elephant(s)

Something that sits in the corner of a room where meaningful conversations take place. You can't talk about it but it's so big it affects everyone. What's the elephant in your room? Impending job cuts, last year's failed initiative or that slight smell of broccoli from the guy in Compliance? Don't ask zookeepers, though. They may actually have an elephant in their room. I made that mistake once. And one time I told this group, 'Well, it's hardly rocket science, is it?' Then I remembered I was at the Luton Federation of Rocket Scientists.

Elevator Pitch

Selling your story in the time it takes for an elevator ride. Imagine the scenario. By chance, you are stuck with your CEO or a big potential customer. The doors shut. You press 4 (or 34 if you are in America or Canary Wharf). You have forty-five seconds or less to impress them. However, the reality is we tend to avoid eye contact – or indeed any sort of contact – hopeful that we can maintain a safe distance. I shun this cowardly approach and have done my elevator pitch on many occasions. Here it is:

'Hi, my name is L. Vaughan Spencer. I can change your life and that of your company. Look me in the eye right now and tell me there isn't something about your own career or relationships (professional or personal) that couldn't be upgraded. And can you press the button for floor 4 please?'

In terms of others' reactions, you have to take the rough with the smooth … here are the kinds of things that have happened:

It wasn't who I thought it was.

They all got out while I was halfway through.

He told me to shut up.

She pushed me out of the elevator.

It turned out that she was a life coach as well and she offered to help me with my issues.

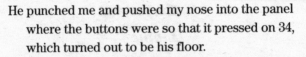

He punched me and pushed my nose into the panel
where the buttons were so that it pressed on 34,
which turned out to be his floor.

That said, on several occasions (well, 4.7 per cent) there
was a successful outcome. They took my BUZZNESS CARD and
signed up for a course. That fraction is surely worth going
for, even if you may end up with a bruised ego or nose.

Write Your Elevator Pitch Here

I am great because ....
....
....
You should buy these because ....
....
....
Please go out with me because ....
....
....

Elf

I have developed the system of Personal Self-Enhancement
(PSE). Let's look at that word 'Self'. Take away the first letter
and what do you have?

ELF

Is that you? If so, it's time to say no to your Inner Elf – a mis-
chievous little sprite in your head undermining your Personal
Self-Enhancement. Think of it this way:

Embedded
Lippy
Foe

Yes, your inner foe is busy saying things like:

You're no good.

Nobody likes you.

You don't deserve success.

Frankie B is with your ex-wife.

We call this Negative Self-Talk or ELF-TALK. Tell the Elf to go away! Expel the Elf.

Say Yes to Your True Self!

Elf-Talk

What your internal nay-sayer does. Think of an internal yea-sayer. It may help to call him or her Lil Vo. Think of a tiny version of me.

Email

Both a curse and a blessing. I could spend my whole day dealing with email. I must get over ten a day! Without the spam, it would make things much more manageable. Make sure you don't send an email when you're angry. I've lost several clients this way. And friends. And romantic partners. I should have waited till the morning, or at least until leaving her house.

I suggest that one day a week you leave it alone. How about Friday? I call it E-Free Friday. So you can dress down *and* not do email on a Friday. Instead of email you can focus on important other stuff, such as:

Having meaningful interfaces with colleagues.

Smiling at passers-by.

Tidying your desk.

Phoning your mother.

Having an anger management session.

Making a list of people to email first thing Monday morning.

That's the sort of thing I used to do when I could access my emails. Now every day is e-free. If you've sent me an email lately, I'm sorry I haven't replied. Call me. Once I can get Nikki back in for an appraisal, I can ask her for the password for my webmail account. I went to that internet café today but got hassled by those French exchange students. They challenged me to take them on at Frappez les Baguettes – a violent video game as it turned out. I got 'null pointes'.

Emailstrom

When you're faced with just too much email. Maybe you've just returned from holiday. Maybe there's been a crisis. Your inbox is bulging with curt or lengthy responses brimming with anger or fear and copied to anyone and everyone. Do you read the latest first? Or do you try to retrace the story chronologically? Neither. Pick up the phone.

Talk – Don't Type!

Talk to people. Find the person who sent the most recent rant. Give them a hug, a glass of water and some sweeties. Ask what's been happening. Sort it out. Then delete most of the emails without reading.

It's always better to talk than to email. Exceptions include:

☆ Late at night when you've had a great idea for a module on a training course and want to let someone know immediately. It's better than ringing. (I learned this to my cost. One Talent Development Manager was not happy at being rung at 2 a.m. about my idea for the Dolphin & Cheese Role-Play Ice-Breaker. It seems not everyone is as committed to the WAR ON TALENT as me.)

☆ Extricating oneself from difficult encounters (romantic, dental or tennis-related).

☆ Sending spreadsheets. It's just not the same on the phone.

Case Study

At one organisation we instituted the E-Free Friday and it was painful. People had forgotten how to communicate face-to-face. There were tears and fights. In the end, to balance things up, we had to institute Email Monday, when they had to send emails and weren't allowed to speak to each other. That hospital is doing really well now.

Emotion

Vital in today's fast-moving business environment (FMBE). You need passion. You need to swim in the Ocean of Emotion.

> *Dealing with emotional crises*
> *Is not easy*
> *Even if you're a Pisces.*
> *I'm not a goat,*
> *I just need to emote.*

Tamma Chookworth, *Songs for Succeeders*, Vol. 6

(lyrics reproduced by kind permission)

I have to deal almost constantly with emotion. Every day people get angry with me. But you don't make eggs without breaking an omelette. I'm pushing people to achieve their potential, so I have to take the rough with the smooth. My chin can take them both. It's been rough and it's been smooth and it's had plenty of omelette on it. The source of your emotions is You. That's right – You. You have the power to choose whether you allow in the eggs or keep them outside yourself. You have the power to select a positive response, no matter how horrid people are or if they tug your ponytail (especially those French exchange students at the internet café). And words can help. I call it the Question of the Toxic Tongue or the Tonic Tongue. It's your choice …

Is Yours a Toxic Tongue or a Tonic Tongue?

Emotional Intelligence

Not just being good at math and stuff but understanding people and what makes them tick. It's important to be nice and to say please and thank you. Check out my book *Irrational Intelligence*, a best-seller in parts of Saskatchewan.

If you are in a LEADERSHIP/HR/PDB position, here's how to deal with emotional problems at work:

Problem	Emotionally Intelligent Succeeder Intervention
Facing marital break-up	Day off
Lost a relative	Day off
Lost a parent	Two days off
Thinking you're not good enough	Cuddle
Angry	Succeeder Anger-Management Module
Birthday whip-round for somebody you don't know	Give £3, or £5 if there's no change

For Emotional Intelligence, sometimes the shorthand EQ is used, as opposed to IQ. However, neither is as important as your SQ (Succeeder Quotient).

Empathy Economy

First there was the Industrial Revolution. Then there was the Knowledge Revolution. Now there is the 'L-Volution'. Forget the Information Age – think Empathy Economy! Empathy is vital in LEADERSHIP, teamwork and when you FIRE someone. I'm always creating empathy with my clients, and that requires plenty of sacrifices on my part, though I draw the line at nudity, generally speaking. Think of empathy as M-Path-ee, the Path to M – the path to MOTIVITALITY. We can help you put the M into Pathy. Bring the *real you* to work. If you don't know how to do that, sign up for 'The Real Me' Workshop and we'll tell you who the real you is.

Enabler

What a leader should be. Come to think of it, so should a parent or an uncle. My father never thought I would amount to much but look at me now – running a global business and owner of my own car. Yet my sister Veronica is still the golden girl. Why? Just because she's running her own beauty salon? (It's called Bee You Tee. They were going to spell it B-U-T but that didn't look good.) Or is it because she has a son and heir – Liam? Well, I think of all the SUCCEEDERS I've created across the world, and in Watford, as my children. In some ways, it was as painful as real childbirth. MOTIVITALITY is the placenta. The umbilical cord is the Ramada Jarvis Hotel in Watford.

Encore Career

After a very successful career business, some buzzness folk open a second chapter – maybe running a social enterprise, or charity. This is what L-Vo is doing with the whole SUC-CEEDER phenomenon, after blazing a trail in chilled distribution. Having created the SUCCEEDER empire, my appetite is not yet quenched. Wouldn't it be great to have a Succeeder Institute in Africa, where people are so tired and thirsty?

Energy Vacuum (aka Drain-Storm)

He (or she – let's not be sexist here) sucks all the energy out of a room, no matter how big, no matter how many people. You know the type; may well be in a LEADERSHIP position. It is impossible to continue a productive meeting with this sort of person. Quite often he is the ELEPHANT in the room. Strategies to cope:

1. Don't invite them.
2. If they do turn up, nip out and set fire to something near a smoke alarm. Reconvene the meeting somewhere they can't find.
3. Conduct the meeting in French, or any language they may not understand.
4. Ensure they get promoted so they are too important to come.

Note: Option 4 is the one most commonly used. The process gets repeated further up the ladder until they find that they no longer need go to any internal meetings – just external ones. Let the customer bear the brunt!

Entrepreneur

The Captain of Capitalism. The Bombardier of Buzzness. The Engine of Enterprise. The Storm Trooper of Succeediness. Without entrepreneurs, we'd be awash in a sea of management mediocrity. Generally they are trying to make up for a bad relationship with their father. So if you want your offspring to be the entrepreneurs of the future, Dads, you know what to do!

Entrepreneuse

A female ENTREPRENEUR.

[*Ned*: How do you think I am doing so far in appealing to the female reader? Should I do more about shoes, handbags, men's lack of commitment and Moira Stuart?]

Envelope

Something for pushing (see BOUNDARY). Also useful for putting letters and documents in when posting.

E-Succeeder

A SUCCEEDER using the internet.

Executive Burnout

I nearly had this. So I stopped. I got off the merry-go-round of mayhem and took a trip around the world. In return for letting my pal Steve run the business (well, he asked me to leave and I gave him the refrigerated van) I got 10 per cent, which at the time didn't seem much, but the world of chilled distribution has moved on … When he sold out for millions several years later, I was sitting pretty.

Experiential Learning

Forget CHALK 'N' TALK; think WALK THE TALK. Experiential Learning is about getting people out of their COMFORT ZONE. They need to get down and dirty, often outdoors in learning courses such as Hide-and-Succeed, Sink-or-Swim and Succeeder Snooker. These are all available for the experiential learner wanting to focus on issues of LEADERSHIP, Teamwork, Courage, Strategy or Snooker. Here are times and prices:

Hide-and-Succeed £46.00 (£90 for two) (last weekend of every third month)

Sink-or-Swim £75 + insurance (every Saturday morning. Bring own trunks)

Succeeder Snooker £35 (cues available for hire) at Harpenden Snooker and Knockout Whist Club

Face

Your face is your fortune. Research shows that we can tell how successful a company is simply by looking at the face of its leader. So what to do if your face doesn't fit? Easy. Become a consultant. Or be happy being a number three or lower. What about plastic surgery? Unfortunately, this never works. You just look stupid.

Think Outside The Botox!

Instead, use MOISTURISER and do facial exercises regularly. Check out the SUCCEEDER MAKE YOUR FACE FIT© programme. And think about your Face Furniture – take a look at top celebrity glass-wearers like Kate Silverton of BBC *Breakfast*.

Failure

Thomas Watson, the founder of IBM, said, 'If you want to increase your success rate, double your failure rate.' That has certainly been my approach. I have managed to find failure where others have not. I couldn't have been such a success if I hadn't failed time and time again. Look at the great failures of history. Julius Caesar couldn't get a girl-friend. Einstein couldn't get a job – except as a librarian. Abraham Lincoln – shot in the box at the theatre. Ouch. And Bono – he *still* hasn't found what he's looking for. As a kid, I used to be rubbish at spelling. Who'd have guessed I'd go on to invent the life-coaching science of SPELLOLOGY©? Here's an example: if you Fall, you get up, and Fail is just one letter different. So what's stopping you? Change a different letter and Fail becomes Sail. Without sailing close to the wind, you'll never weather the storm. Aye-aye, Cap'n, and all aboard! Go away, stowaway. Get on board and take it to the bridge.

Fail doesn't mean what you think it means. Re-frame it, and it becomes

Future

Advantage

Is

Looming

Mighty powerful, huh? It's one heck of a switch. Are you ready for it? People think you can never become a global guru if you have failed. Well, I did. Those failures were a while back and now SUCCEEDERSHIP© follows me wherever I go. It just turns up – like a good smell. Who would have thought that ugly loon-panted boy with no friends hugging the wall at the disco would become an international com-mentator on Personal Self-Enhancement? I didn't just flirt with failure. I embraced her. I took her home to meet the family.

Now, another kind of failure drives me. Other people's, I mean. I sniff it out and I expunge it. I first realised I could transform lives when I was ten and failed my Cycling Proficiency Test. That's when I realigned my name. I became Vaughan. V is for Victory, Vitality and Vanity; perfect. L is for Leslie; not so perfect. Of course, there have been some failures since then. Divorce could be seen as a failure, yet I took it as an opportunity to meet more ladies.

Dare to Fail. Make It Your Holy Grail!

Write a List of All Your Failures Here

1.

2.

3.

4.

5.

6.

7.

8.

9.

10.

There is another page at the back for you to continue if necessary (see page 245).

Why not come on our SUCCEEDER Failure Course? Don't worry if you've been before. There's a 10 per cent discount as part of your 'Frequent Failure' loyalty programme.

Fear

Fear is good. Fear ensures self-preservation. The only fears we are born with are those of loud noise and bright lights and presented curses. So watch out for a lion with a torch. The problem comes when we learn other fears. What do you fear? To help you, I'll let you know what I fear:

Failure
Humiliation
Rejection
Lions
Electro-magnetic radiation
Prison
Crocodiles
Loneliness
Rancid meat

I could go on. Spend a few minutes thinking about what you fear. To make it easier, I have suggested some categories. Fill in your specific fears for each one:

People . . . .
Creepy-crawlies . . . .
Inner Feelings . . . .
Modes of Transport . . . .
Music . . . .
Ally McCoist . . . .
Invisible Things . . . .
Philosophical Concepts . . . .
Tiny Things . . . .

Baddies in *Doctor Who* (Daleks, Cybermen, Yetties) ....

. . . .

The point is that once we know our fears, we can overcome them. Let them guide you, and overcome them one by one, apart from the ones of loud noise and bright lights.

You'll Never Get the All-Clear from Fear!

Federation of Canadian Life Coaches

The professional body for those who want to be life coaches in Canada. I used to be Assistant Treasurer until a clique hounded me out for no good reason. Anyway, I offered to pay back the money.

Feedback

A great method for improving performance is 360-degree feedback. People above, below and around you report on your performance. This is an excellent way of collating details of why people don't like you. Well, reader, I go further! I do 720-degree feedback; it's like 360-degree feedback – only more!

> *For Feedback a-Plenty*
> *You Need Seven-Twenty!*

I often go and talk about myself to people who've never even met me. And their feedback is always refreshingly candid.

Some people say, 'There is no failure, only feedback.' Well, I can tell you that L-Vo has had lots of that kind of feedback, but it made him stronger. I'm only hoping that applies to the feedback I received last night. I took the manageress of the Luton Nail Salon to La Grande Bouche, my favourite bistro. At the end of the meal, I asked her to fill in a short questionnaire, so I could build on things for future interfaces. Categories included Clothes, Food, Questioning and Listening Skills, and Humour Levels. Just regular stuff for a first date. It didn't go down well, though not nearly as badly as when I gave her the feedback form I'd completed on her BEHAVIOURS. I gave her the maximum five for most things (Hair, Punctuality, Dress Sense, Focus, Smiling) but I couldn't overlook the soup incident. She stormed out.

Remember, feedback is a gift. Accept gifts with grace. This is what I tell my students and clients as I point out where they are going wrong. On my travels in search of personal and BUZZNESS enlightenment, I have studied many tribes. The AYCH-ARE have no word for 'failure' and thus no concept of it. But they do have seventy-three words for feedback.

To Succeed You Need Feed(back)!

Feminism

Not surprisingly, I am a committed feminist with a real belief in the strength of women (or Girl Power, as I prefer to call it!). But I have noticed that ladies don't always get a fair crack of the whip. So I run a Ladies' Empowerment Workshop. No more shrinking violets! Sometimes we guys may not even be aware of our own unconscious sexism. Through bitter experience I have learned that there are some words to be avoided in even the most postmodern company.

Words to Avoid If You Don't Want to Annoy the Ladies

Poppet	Sweetheart	Darling
Lovey	Honey	Sweetie

Some of these words can irritate even women who have a sense of humour. So avoid using them in the business context (unless involved in a ROLE PLAY in a safe and fully facilitated environment where this may be required). This is why I use Neutered Language© – a non-gender-specific SUC-CEEDER language for the sensitive businessperson of either sex. So NL© is a great way of checking. Right, girls? Here are some examples:

Wrong	Right
Pretty	Energised
Flirt	Network
'Fit'	Fit
Ugly	Experienced
Phwoar!	Hello
Humourless	Task-oriented

Feng Shui

Eastern way of looking at energy and furniture and stuff. The geo-astro-magnetics of decor. If you want good luck, avoid pointy things. Keep a mirror by the front door to scare away DRAGONS (and I don't mean the ones on *Dragons' Den*. Well, actually, I do. They may want a share of your business!). And burglars. Keep a wind chime above your steering wheel. In my own flat I have a water feature in the bathroom. It doubles as a toilet but I always keep the lid down. My wardrobe is in the clothes corner and I've built a little mountain of bricks on my roof terrace so bad energy bounces off my back door and goes into that estate agent's next door.

See also TONG SHUI© – *the Feng Shui of hair*.

Fire

Sir Alan Sugar simply says, 'You're fired!' We all know it's nothing like that in real life. It's much more brutal. You're escorted back to your desk, given a bin liner and told to remove all personal belongings, then marched out to reception. Well, that's what happened to me at the call centre. So how do we make it more humane?

Top Tips for 'Letting Someone Go'

1   Choose an appropriate time. Friday at five o'clock will ruin their weekend.
2   Smile.
3   Find a suitable room. Not an open-plan office, the factory floor or the toilet. Find a nice quiet room and have some gentle music playing, or, better still, their favourite track (this did unfortunately backfire with one company, where the soon-to-be-ex-employee's favourite song was 'When Will I See You Again?' by the Three Degrees).
4   Make out it's not their fault. Say something like, 'It's not you. It's us.'
5   Smile.
6   Have some useful information ready. For example, the bus timetable so they can get the next one and be home soon, and the phone number of the JobCentre or the Samaritans.
7   Don't say that you feel bad – unless you are a very good actor.
8   If you think they will take it badly, have someone large on hand and remove heavy objects from the room.
9   Remember to keep smiling.

Firewalk*

Walking on hot coals to show you are a SUCCEEDER to actually physically transcend the fear of failure. For HEALTH AND SAFETY reasons, this isn't a good idea on most carpets in the average workplace or seminar environment (as I discovered to my cost at the Ramada Jarvis in Watford!). To achieve HOCUS-FOCUS, it's best to intone a MOTI-MANTRA while doing this, something like, 'It's not hurting! It's not hurting!'

Fizzness

As in 'I love the fizzness of business.' There is very little that can match the pure, unalloyed out-of-body pleasurable zing of business at its best. Mmmm, I feel good just writing those words. Pass me my mobile right now and let me network.

Make Your Biz Have Fizz!

Flexible Working

I'm never not working. Sometimes I'm up at 4 a.m., just buzzing with biz. I have new ideas for the SUCCEEDER phenomenon. For example, this morning I was working on designs for a Succeeder Steering Wheel for on-the-move MOTIVITALITY. It's one thing to listen in-car to a Succeedy CD, but this will really put the cat on the tin lid. And don't think that means I'm knocking off after lunch. Well, actually I will, but that's because I'm playing tennis with Nikki's dad, hoping

---

*Note for PDB professionals: After one go at this, I decided never again, but if you are going to do it, get people to sign a waiver along the lines of: 'I am fully aware that I could suffer extreme injury, including burns and big damage, physical or mental, like being burned.' Some salesmen from Luton & Beds Insurance did end up in hospital, ironically! Now I use the BALLOON OF DESTINY© instead.

he can persuade her to come back. This time I will offer her flexible working. She's been bellyaching about it for a while. She can forgo the APPRECIATION HOUR and WARM-UP and knock off around teatime.

Followership

LEADERSHIP is the big buzzword in business now. Leaders are knee-deep in leadership courses. But not everyone can be a Leader. You need Followers. The problem with business today is that there are too many cooks and not enough Indian takeaways, if you get my meaning!

Consultants talk about Leadership Bandwidth to mean how wide the leadership in your organisation is. But is it? ... Is it time to increase your Followership Bandwidth? The CEO's Leadership Footprint may be too big. That's why the L. Vaughan Spencer Foundation is running Followership courses, with modules including:

How to Do What You're Told

How to Avoid Using Your Initiative

Find Your Inner Yes-Man

Follow My Leader

The Yellow Brick Road: A Case Study (Are You a
    Cowardly Lion, a Tin Man or a Friend of Dorothy?)

Your Instincts: How Best to Ignore Them

Nodding: Making It Believable

How Brown Is Your Nose?

Then, for advanced students, we offer *UnderLing-uis-tics: The Science of Talking to Your Boss* and *Acquiesce Is Best.*

Food

Vital in today's fast-moving business environment (FMBE).
See ALPHABET DIET.

According to research by Professor Trankin, lack of food
leads directly to feeling hungry for 100 per cent of people.

Hippocrates said, 'Make food your medicine and medicine your food.' He was right, even though he's dead now.
Many people who have been on the SUCCEEDER Workshop
have changed their lives. Sometimes, it's just a matter of
changing what you eat. Let me tell you about a guy named
Charles. He now testifies at my workshops:

*'I thought that I had it all … car, house, family, fancy job.
But really I had nothing. I was nothing. L-Vo showed me
that deep down I was unhappy. My face was unmoisturised.
Oh, sure I was running my own firm, making a million a
year. But L-Vo showed me, by pointing out all my flaws,
that really I was a failure. We totally overhauled my life –
starting with my diet. So now I eat chicken, cress, carrot,
cheese, Chinese food and chocolate-covered things. I live
alone in a tent. My wife and children and friends didn't
understand but L-Vo does.'*

Charles, former CEO Brainbox Software

His life is much better now. Simpler, certainly.

Of course, it is no surprise to me that Frankie B (see how
he's trying to sound a bit like Jazzie B (OBE) of Soul II Soul?)
He should 'Keep on Movin'' or get 'Back to Life, Back to
Reality') is trying to cash in on my work in this area. He now
has his own line of organic food bars – the 'Life-Changer Lite
Oat Loaf'. It's got all sorts of different things mixed in – like
apricot and dried flowers and even something called Xanthan

gum, whatever that is. Who's going to eat that – apart from someone called Xavier?

Foreign

Even though the British invented business we aren't the only ones doing it. The Americans got rather good at it too and now the rest of the world is catching up. Other cultures have plenty to teach us about BUZZNESS. The Japanese, obviously, have lots of useful words. So that's why I am studying it, along with Chinese, Russian, Indian and Brazilian. So far I can only say 'hello' and 'thank you', but I reckon that's all you need to negotiate in any language (along with confidence and good eye contact). I am sure the London Olympics will give me a great chance to globalise the SUCCEEDER phenomenon. I have already written to Lord Sebastian Coe to ask if I can hand out Succeeder flyers during the opening ceremony.

But here are two very useful foreign phrases:

French: *'Plus ça change, plus c'est la même chose'* … 'Oh no, here comes another change programme.'

Australian: *'No worries, mate'* … 'We have indeed conducted Due Diligence.'

One time I was giving a talk on LEADERSHIP in Greece and the title got translated as 'Don't Be Needed, Be Succeeded', which isn't what most leaders want to hear.

Franchise

This is where you buy the chance to run someone else's business for them. You buy a licence and they give you the where-withall. I did this myself once when times were hard, with

Tunes4Toddlers, an international pre-school music franchise, but I stopped after a week because I was exhausted and the kids kept pulling my ponytail.

However, we are now looking into franchising the SUC-CEEDER experience across the world. Would you like to be your local representative? We have very reasonable terms. Already, Petros (or Pete, as he likes to be known) has bought the franchise for Greece, and we've been working on creating Hellenic versions of the Succeedy concepts. It's not easy, especially with the ALPHABET DIET, because they don't use proper letters.

Friendship Audit

Are you too busy – rushed off your feet with no time to do what you really, really want, yet you end up seeing friends you don't really like? Time for a Friendship Audit, an inventory of your personal life, if you will. Cut out the deadwood or the 'past-their-sell-by' relationships. Time to be hard-nosed. What use is this person to you? Think about your friends one by one from a business perspective:

Merger opportunities (Is romance on the cards?).
Investment/cash-flow (Do they pay more than their
    share when we are together?).
Market profile (I know this bloke from school, but he's
    always short of money, and tries to get off with any
    female companion I have, yet he plays in a village
    cricket team full of highly networthy types and
    potential SUCCEEDERS).

So, write some notes on each person. It will be worth it. Think laterally as well. The friendship/BUZZNESS SYNERGY paradigm can work the other way round too. For example, you might be able to outsource some of the activities connected with relationships. Do I really need to buy a birthday gift for the wife? Could I not use this as a sponsorship opportunity for a valued customer? I often allowed clients to sponsor presents for my wife -- one Valentine's Day was sponsored by a ten-pin bowling alley. We simply had to wear their branded polo shirts all day and we had a free lane that evening!

See also ROOM WORKER.

Games

A great way to break the ice at a conference and to illustrate
how business operates. So we play Twister when working on
Strategy, Kerplunk for Planning and Monopoly for Corporate
Governance. Here are some more, with their applications:

British Bulldog – going head-to-head with a competitor
'Off-Ground Tick' – reducing complexity in the supply
    chain
Human Chess – acquisitions
Draughts – coping with logistics
Piggy-in-the-Middle – overcoming silo mentality
Trivial Pursuit – instead of a job interview
Scrabble – SPELLOLOGY
Risk – risk
Cluedo – finding out who's been murdered in the
    company, where and how

Gaming

I am working on a SUCCEEDER interactive game – Grand Theft
L-Vo. Your avatar is a consultant parachuted into a company

where morale is low. You've got to save it by going through the Labyrinth of Change – dealing with mortal foes from Finance, HR, Business Affairs and Operations, as well as internal and external saboteurs, who are all hiding behind filing cabinets, partition walls and burnt-out cars. You must try to get to the highest level – X-TREME MOTIVATOR.

Also there is another – your career as a 3-D video game. In Steer Your Career you have to negotiate obstacles – INTER-VIEWS, promotions, conferences, budgets, pitches, overrunning projects, GARDENING LEAVE, overseas postings, APPRAISALS and changing markets – armed only with a machine gun and a pack of emergency mythical mentors and shape-shifters (e.g. Mr Moisturise, the Tiger of Tong Shui, the Diet Dragon, the Phoenix of Failure, the Gangsta Griffin and the Monster of Motivitality). We are hoping to talk to the makers of Guitar Hero 4 about creating Business Hero, charting the Hero's Business Journey (HBJ).

Gamma Male

Happy being mediocre (compare ALPHA MALE). Doesn't want to upset the apple cart. Knocks off early, doesn't rush with that project, not looking for promotion, not keen to get higher than number sixty-seven in the pecking order. Statistically speaking, these guys are vital. If everyone were a leader, then there would be nobody left to lead. The danger comes when a Gamma Male is taken by surprise and shunted into a position of LEADERSHIP (e.g. if he is tall) and has to pretend to be an Alpha. Most organisations are full of such examples.

I was a Gamma Male, I will happily admit. That's how I can feel your pain so easily. I was nine. The police took me in. I'd fallen in with a bad crowd and failed my Cycling

Proficiency Test. I was at my lowest ebb. Someone's space-hopper had gone missing and I was the prime suspect. I came face-to-face with my own dark side. I had to wait a quarter of an hour at the police station for my mum to arrive. They were the longest fifteen minutes of my life. I know how it must feel to be on Death Row. I vowed never to be in that position. I blamed Roger Futtock.

Gardening Leave

Where you go and work for someone else but aren't allowed to start yet. You have to wait around doing nothing while your knowledge becomes out of date (your ex-employers hope). But does anyone actually spend this time gardening? Wouldn't it be better called:

Sitting around leave?

Golfing leave?

Working-for-your-new-employer-surreptitiously leave?

Gardening may be the new rock 'n' roll, but who would you rather have on your team – Billy Idol or Alan Titchmarsh? A 'Rebel Yell' may be all very well, but it won't keep the greenfly off! Check out my book *Garden Your Way to the Top*. Every organisation needs pruning now and then, you sure need some fertiliser and we all need watering. (Are you properly hydrated? Remember, eight glasses of water a day or you'll wilt in the midday sun of commercial competition, hopelessly unmoisturised and outflanked by an Evian expert.)

Give Good Meeting (GGM)

Vital in today's fast-moving business environment (FMBE). If you're no good at meetings you're no good at business.

Tired of meetings – tired of life! Except most of us can't GGM. We expect meetings to be productive and to agree to specific actions, especially what we want to happen. Wrong.

Meetings Are Not Forums for Action!

They are forums for inaction, politics, fear-mongering, posturing and flirting. All of which are vital in business – without a doubt. So here are some suggestions for radicalising and energising your meetings:

☆ Dispense with chairs. Everyone must stand.

☆ Everyone is only allowed to say three things in the entire meeting

☆ Every quarter of an hour stop the meeting and everyone has to dance to 'The Birdie Song' – with actions.

If however, your organisation persists with the traditional approach to meetings, you can still be a Meeting Machiavelli. Sit back in your not-so-comfortable-not-very-ergonomic-chair, pour the coffee that's been waiting for ever in that pot thing that spills as it pours, avoid the pink wafers and boiled sweets, knuckle down to the agenda and play the game. Here are the rules:

Top Tips for Meetings

☆ Sit opposite the chairman/woman. Give them good eye contact. Maybe the occasional wink. If she or he is right-handed, put up your right hand when you have a point. Vice versa for left-handers, unless you've got a big plaster on that hand. If they are ambidextrous, get up and move during the meeting.

☆ Work out who the most negative person in the room is and keep passing them notes saying things like 'Well done', 'Good point' and 'I don't want my biscuit. Would you like it?'

☆ Agree to nothing.

☆ Pass the biscuits around, especially when your enemy is talking.

☆ Agree with your enemy on one thing very enthusiastically so as to unnerve them.

See also MEET-ERCISE *and* MEETINGS.

Globalisation

Globalisation is becoming a worldwide phenomenon. More people graduated in India last year than have graduated in America and Britain since the third century and they can all speak better English. Cross-cultural business etiquette needs to be learned. Be careful how you name your product. For example, I found out that SUCCEEDER in Greek means something very rude, so I'm working with a phrase that translates as 'one who sits comfortably in a field of success', which the man in Café Olympus in Harpenden told me would work. I must have mispronounced it the other day, when I was speaking to a Greek tycoon and he had me escorted from the airport.

In some cultures, giving someone a business card is tantamount to calling their mother a non-achiever, whereas in others they are honour-bound to punch you if you *don't*! And you have to take presents – according to my friend Frederick, who was filling me in on all this stuff late last night at the tennis club over a glass or two of sparkling wine. Apparently cheese always works well. You have to wear the right clothes (e.g. the right tie/shirt and sandal/sock combo) and the Japanese like you to show them the waistband of your pants. Thanks, Frederick, for all the above – can't wait to put it into action.

Goals

Are important – and not just in soccer! Do you have any? Time for a Personal Inventory. Here's the 8-Step Programme, which is the same as the 2-Step one but it takes a bit longer:

Step 1 Buy a notebook.
Step 2 Buy a pen.
Step 3 Go home.
Step 4 Once inside the home, take out the pen and paper and write down your Goals.
Step 5 Read your Goals.
Step 6 Feel free to change them.
Step 7 OK now?
Step 8 Start achieving them.

Did you write down your Goals when you were young? Recently I found mine, aged fifteen:

Make a lot of money.
Own a big red car.
Get off with Nicole Futtock.

Sadly, I never got that red car. I've got a big silver one now, with a sunroof. Charles doesn't need it any more, so it seems a shame to waste it. I've travelled the world, visiting primitive peoples, initially to spread the word about the possibilities for refrigerated transport. Pretty soon I was the one learning from them. I removed the word 'Failure' from my dictionary – a little unfortunate because, in tearing it out, I removed the word on the reverse of the page, which included 'Faithful'. Which brings us back to Nicole – she wasn't. And now I've pasted Failure back in my dictionary because it makes me strong – *see* FAILURE.

So why Goals? Because a Goal:

Gives
Off
Aspirational
Light

You may have heard of the GROW or SMART models, but I have developed a better one. Your goals must be:

Particular
Relevant
Attainable
Time-bound

So, if ever you are lacking HOCUS-FOCUS, think of L-Vo and think PRAT.

Guiltoholic

One who is addicted to guilt. They won't listen to others in their search of regret and often try to infect them with the condition. Still, it can't be all bad. Just think of the great songs about guilt – 'Guilty' by Classix Nouveaux and George Michael's 'Guilty Feet Have No Rhythm'. I've certainly found that to be true.

Case Study

There was a chief executive (let's call him Charles) who was racked by guilt because he had made so much money. I soon cleared that through a 'Wilt the Guilt' session. It involved me shouting, him crying and some Plasticine. Now he doesn't feel guilty at all, because he has given all his money to the SUCCEEDER INSTITUTE.

Guyliner

Eyeliner for men. Useful for certain situations, such as giving a presentation under very bright lights, at Halloween and dealing with political canvassers.

Hair

Are you Hair aware? Hair awareness is vital in today's fast-moving business environment (FMBE). Without a doubt. Many organisations these days have FENG SHUI consultants. What about a TONG SHUI© consultant? Tong Shui© is the ancient art of hair alignment that I invented. Overlook it at your peril! Just as clothes say everything about you, so does the energy of your hair. Many CEOs neglect Rule One of SUCCEEDEROLOGY©:

Respect Your Hair!

I coach many senior leaders who are eager to navigate the maze of mayhem that is modern business. I always start with the basics:

☆ Is that side-parting right for you?
☆ Could those sideburns be given a little more encouragement?
☆ What about a ponytail? (It can enhance the prowess of many a forty-plus executive.)

Hair can make or break your career. If you are the picture, it's your frame. Would you put a Picasso in a clip frame from

Poundstretchers? Hair gives us vital information about future business partners or would-be employees. If it's dank and lank, you know you won't get to the first base of BUZZNESS. If it's got bounce and shine, you will be first in line. Hair is the one body part we can shape or colour to express our personalities and our business intentions. It speaks volumes in the Cosmic Conversation of Commerce. No wonder that £17 billion is spent on hair products every year in the UK. I think.

Here are some modules available in our 'Success Through Coiffure' podcast series:

Beard: Weird or Feared?

Does a Fringe Unhinge?

Is a Bob Just the Job?

Backcombing in Middle Management

Feather-cut or Bed-head: Which Is Better in Private Equity?

Sideburns: Yes or No? (If so, Should They Be Those Ones That Come to a Sharp Point?)

Get your hair right and the rest will follow. That's why I wear a ponytail – it keeps the dragon of failure off my back. He's always ready to creep up behind us. If you really don't want hair at the back, a collar will deter him. One of my clients got rid of his 'comb-over' and the next day he won a new contract for supplying filing cabinets to a major road-haulage company. *And* met a lady. Don't tell me that's a coincidence, reader! Hair is a cosmic conduit to your aura. It protects you from the evil rays of the psychic ozone. Coiffure and fortune are closely aligned. Hence the phrases 'Bad hair day' and 'Keep your hair on.' Some say baldness implies failure – yet it need not. Lenin and Mussolini had success – in their own kind of way – as did Churchill. He showed the Power of the Hat, along with General de Gaulle, Che Guevara and U2's the Edge.

Head-Hunting

This is the practice among primitive tribes of collecting the heads of enemies as trophies. A modern version exists involving secretive executive breakfasts, but otherwise it has changed little. For advice on what to do if one of your staff has been head-hunted, *see* TALENT MANAGEMENT. I'm wondering if Nikki has been head-hunted. I have been myself on a few occasions. I did take an informal brunch at the Hilton Garden Inn, Luton North. There was loose talk about heading up the Dunstable Enterprise Forum. In the end I decided I'd rather stay in the cut-and-thrust of the private sector. And I didn't like the woman. She didn't seem to appreciate having to give me a ride back to the office via the dry-cleaner's after I had shunned her somewhat clumsy romantic overtures. Or my ringing up several times during the following week to discuss other options. Or my going to her house.

Health and Safety

To stop companies killing their employees by mistake. But in business difficult choices must be made. It's a judgement call where shareholder value could be affected. That's what insurance is for. And the courts. We run a course called 'Safety Is Not A Luxury, It's A Lifestyle'. For many, safety is a bread-and-butter issue, especially if the bread lands butter-side-down. We get people to chant the MOTI-MANTRA 'Your Safety Is My Safety!' and it seems to work, though one man did end up punching another who was chanting it too loudly in his ear at that librarians' AWAYDAY.

Hello

My favourite word – apart from YES and MOTIVITALITY, SUC-
CEEDER and *Steve Wright in the Afternoon*. It's about a new
beginning, the dawn of a new chapter or a new relationship.
To increase your good karma, say hello to a stranger every
day (but first make sure they don't have a weapon). This
could also be good for NETWORKING possibilities, but make
sure that the stranger appears to be in a reasonably sound
financial position first. Avoid those who may be a drain on
your resources.

Hocus-Focus

See BLOOD, SWEAT AND TEARS.

Hot-Desking

Vital in today's fast-moving business environment (FMBE).
This is a situation in which there are fewer desks than people.
It's based on the assumption that on most days a percentage
of people don't turn up for work. They may have MEETINGS,
they may be 'working from home' or it may be their child's
school sports day, again. Every morning, it's a case of first
come, first served. Obviously, complexity creeps in. There's
'Hotelling', whereby you can ring up in advance to reserve a
particular desk if you are working on a specific project. Just
like a real hotel, if you're lucky, your company will lay on a
mini-bar, a trouser press and a turn-down service at night
with a chocolate on the pillow. In return, however, you are
expected to do some work.

At one firm where I consulted I found a guy still wander-
ing around at 4 p.m. trying to find a desk. When I checked the
car park, I spotted loads of people in their cars working on

their laptops. I found that the boss was so keen on Hot-Desking that he had reduced the number of desks to twelve for a workforce of 100. Their mobile phone bills were huge. At another place, I spotted a guy who couldn't remember where 'today's desk' was. Three hours later, he realised he was in the wrong building.

Research says that this ain't great for teamwork, because your team is scattered far and wide. If teams go three days without gathering, they get unhappy and productivity suffers. So I tell leaders to bring their teams together every three days, even if it's just to say hi. Problem is, it's hard to find a place to meet, so they usually end up in the toilets …

Ice-Breaker

A great way to break the ice, which means putting people who are highly stressed about doing communal activities at their ease. You do this by forcing them to take part in group exercises. I have various games and warm-ups I use to really put people at their ease. Here are some of my most effective exercises:

1. In pairs, people share their most embarrassing moment. Then your partner tells the room and we vote on what we think was the most embarrassing.

2. In pairs again, people share their Biggest Business Triumph (BBT). Whether it was completing a deal, getting that photocopying done or managing to start a laundry business in Romania doesn't matter. It just gets people talking openly and freely about business – the Great Uniter.

3. A group game. Everyone is assigned an animal. They have to make the noise of that animal and find the other cats/dogs/cows/sheep/otters/squirrels in the room. It's such fun and really breaks down barriers. Though some people do need reminding that they don't need to keep

making the noises for the rest of the week, and certainly
not in the hotel sauna or in the hotel corridor outside
my bedroom at three in the morning.

Impactfulness

How can we maintain Impactfulness? In a room full of strangers, how can we make sure they remember us? Many have
found themselves transformed by the SUCCEEDER Body Language and Touching Course©. Starting with Deep-Tissue Ego
Massage (from Cranston and his team of former paramilitaries) and proceeding to Advanced Elbow Strategy, many
have found we can transform an Anxious GUILTOHOLIC into a
Major League ROOM WORKER.

Elissa (not her real name; that's Frances) was painfully
shy. She used to hide in the stationery cupboard for most of
the day, despite being chief executive of a hospital trust.
Now she is a lap dancer and runs 'Assert Yer Booty' courses
for other leaders in the public sector. Of course, our post-
training service recognises that people may relapse. They
can ring the Succeedy Line twenty-four hours a day (calls
charged at £17.53 per minute; check with the bill payer if you
like). This is motivation by phone – or PHONIVATION©. Without
it, Elissa would still be in that cupboard. Are you still stuck
among the paperclips?

Do You Detract or Do You Have Impact?

In-Car Motivitalising

Getting HOCUS-FOCUSed in the car en route to a meeting. Vital
in today's fast-moving business environment (FMBE), where
every second counts. You want to hit the ground running as
soon as the BUZZNESS interface commences, so prepare

yourself in the car (or limo or taxi or train or bus). You may want to chant a MOTI-MANTRA (e.g. 'I am Succeedy, I am Succeedy') or listen to some MOTI-MUSIC (e.g. 'Get Outta My Dreams, Get into My Car' or 'When the Going Gets Tough, the Tough Get Going' or indeed anything by Billy Ocean, though not 'Suddenly'; my wife and I used to play that – it was 'our' song. Now I play 'Love Really Hurts Without You'). I often listen to *Steve Wright in the Afternoon* or Ken Bruce in the morning.

You may like to listen to one of my spoken-word Succeedy CDs, where I tell you that you can be better with the occasional bit of URBAN TRIBAL DRUMMING to keep you awake. We also supply car-friendly coat hangers with motivational messages. For example, 'Put on the Cloak of Confidence'; 'Jump into the Jacket of Joy'; 'This is Your Shirt of Sureness'.

Induction

What they do to you when you start a new job, introducing you to HEALTH AND SAFETY, corporate values and which font you must use. Of course, the official 'vanilla' version of induction is only so much help. I make companies create and deliver an Authentic Induction, which tells you things like:

☆ The name of the Security Guard and his favourite brand of whisky.

☆ Which is the CEO's car.

☆ The company stud and how to avoid him.

☆ Who authorises deviations from company policy: e.g. first-class travel when you're only entitled to economy.

☆ Who does the office seating plan – you don't want to be stuck by the toilets.

☆ How to 'facilitate the promotion to another department' (i.e. instead of firing) of your useless assistant.

☆ How to get access to your boss's calendar so you can arrange your social life for when he or she is away on business/leaving early.

☆ Who allocates secretaries and beanbags – and what their bribe of choice is.

☆ Who runs 'special events' and will be off-loading tickets to all the major sporting events at the last minute when you haven't been able to buy them for genuine corporate entertaining through your 'cost centre' because of the ridiculous mark-up caused by the internal market and everywhere trying to be a cost centre.

Influence

Helping people to understand what they really, really want. Which is usually to buy something from you.

Seven Ways to Influence People

1. Look at their forehead when they are talking.
2. Smile. Give them a wink when nobody is looking.
3. Don't wince when they are talking.
4. Tell them as much as you can about yourself.
5. Make a point of pointing out where they are wrong.
6. Make them understand how influential and important you are.
7. Give them some cheese.

Information

Did you know that, thanks to the internet, more words have been published since you started reading this book than had been up to the year 2000? This is scary and is leading to information overflow. How can we deal with this Overload Anxiety?

See also OVERLOAD-ANOIA.

Internet

The internet is great, isn't it? I love checking things and emailing friends and sending out my weekly *Succeed-e-Zine*, in which I include Succeedy Snippets and great quotes from great people who've said great things and don't charge for being quoted. People send in their own stories often, so I don't have to write anything. It's also a good way to remind people of all the Succeedy merchandise which is just a click away (Succeedy T-shirts, MOTIVITALITY Mugs and Gangsta Gloves).

If I had to start again, I would certainly think about being a dotcom millionaire. It seems quite easy. I'm thinking of creating a SUCCEEDER Social Network site, where people share stories and pictures of themselves being Succeedy and they pay for the privilege – obviously with the profits going to the SUCCEEDER INSTITUTE to research *BUZZNESS* topics and help my favourite charity, *BUSINESSPEOPLE IN NEED*.

Interviews (Job)

A vital getting-to-know-you session for both parties, like animals sniffing each other out. Does the applicant smell good? Has the employer marked out some top territory?

Top Tips for Interviewers

Watch their eyes – do they seem shifty?

Speak a bit too loudly – does it faze them?

Pretend to make notes as you go, continually breaking eye
    contact. Can they take it?

Top Tips for Interviewees

Warm up – mentally and physically. Do the SUCCEEDER War
    Dance (*see* DANCE).

Wear great CLOTHES.

Give your HAIR its due.

Find out about the company – what it does, for example.

Top Tips for Before the Interview

Don't accept a cappuccino before going in; you'll end with a
    milky choc-moustache or spilling it on your lap.

Always have something ready when they ask at the end,
    'And do *you* have questions?' (A good one is 'Where do
    you see this company in five years' time?' Unless they
    have told you that during the interview, in which case
    ask them, 'Where do you see this company in ten years'
    time?')

Do some IN-CAR MOTIVITALISING – I suggest 'I Love Rock 'n' Roll'
    by Joan Jett and the Blackhearts.

Hire a Person, Not Just a CV!

Intranet

Something like the internet but only people working in the company can access it. It's an electronic version of what used to be called the Noticeboard and has exciting interactive training possibilities. We often go in and Succeederise the intranet of an organisation. Here are some successful features:

☆ Photo Gallery, where employees can upload pictures of colleagues in action under such headings as:
  – Succeeder of the Month
  – A Smile That Takes You the Extra Mile
  – Inappropriate Behaviour Exposed
  – Tong Shui Choice of the Month (interesting hairstyle innovations)

☆ The Biz-Blog, where employees can contribute something along the following lines:
  – Moti-Verse (Succeedy stanzas)
  – What I Learned from My Kids
  – L. Vaughan Spencer is Great Because . . . .
    . . . .
  – I'm Going to Leave Because . . . .
    . . . .

Irritati

Members of the club of irritating people – as exclusive as the glitterati except they don't know they are members.

See also DIFFICULT PEOPLE.

Itis-itis

The overload of diseases that gets us down:

Agenda-itis

Change-itis
Jargon-itis
Meeting-itis
Powerpoint-itis

Anything can become an 'itis'. Or almost anything – nobody ever got L-Vo-itis!

Jargon

[*Ned*: – Under 'jargon' you keep writing 'What people from Norwich do to keep fit.' I presume this is a joke. Humour in business may very well be appropriate in its place. This is a serious business book. I will do humour in my next one.]

Jargon is your friend. Professor Krench found that companies with jargon did 8 per cent better. You can't survive without it. I worked with a firm where they had a 'Drive Out Jargon' campaign. Company well-being took a nose-dive. People were constantly off sick or they left. I led a 'Bring Back the Jargon' change programme, which made everyone feel much more secure. Instead of a swear box, we had a Jargon Jar, where people had to pay a pound if they didn't use the correct nomenclature or TLA. One senior manager ended up having to write a cheque for £453. We gave it to BUSINESSPEOPLE IN NEED.

Jean-Michel Jarre

The L. Vaughan Spencer of Music. Quite simply the best.

Job Description

Very important. So often there is Mission Creep, where you are hired to do one thing and end up doing lots more. What is L-Vo's job description? It's hard to say, as I do so much! I mean, you wouldn't ask Superman for his job description, would you? I guess the best way to describe me is as Business Viagra. I'm an adrenalin surge for any organisation. I'm a kick up the backside with a spiritual slipper. Here's something you can use when writing a job description:

You will do . . . .
lots of interesting sounding things that don't include heavy lifting

You will have these qualifications . . . .
degree to at least 2:1/software skills/Cycling Proficiency Test

You will be reporting to . . . .
very important person

You need to be able to . . . .
write/lead/smile

You will have proven experience . . . .
working under pressure/working in a team/smiling

You will be paid . . . .
the minimum wage/£20k/whatever you ask if you GIVE GOOD MEETING

Job Title

Here are some job titles I have introduced to a number of my client companies to increase morale:

Canteen King

Chief Succeedy Officer

Gangsta Godmother

Keeper of Cash
Operative (Operations)
Princess of Productivity
Project Motivitaliser
Queen of Queries
Vice-President (Success)

These tend to be given in lieu of a salary increase – especially Vice-President.

Journals

I'm the editor of *Success & Succeediness*, which is a fully peer-reviewed semi-quasi-academic journal. If you want to stay abreast of the BUZZNESS Zeitgeist here are some other journals I would recommend:

Abstract of Death
American Olfactory Review
Journal of Supply Chain Solutions and Logistics
    (They have *great* cartoons!)
New England Quarterly Review of Moisturizers
Weird!!

And there are always things in *Tennis Now!* that get my creativising juices going.

Recently I have been interviewed by a journal – *Watford Business Sheet*'s Young Biz Section for teenagers. Here is an extract:

What's your favourite music?

Right now, Rihanna. She's really good. And Duffy. I think he's terrific. Right up there with Jean-Michel Jarre. At the moment I've got Mike and the Mechanics in my car. Not literally! No – on a cassette I taped off my friend Charles.

Fave food?

Being on the Alphabet Diet restricts my choice somewhat. This month I'm on L, so I'm having plenty of Lettuce, and the occasional Luxury Mince Pie from M&S. Next month it's V, so I'll major on Vegetables and Vietnamese food. The following month is S, so the world's my oyster! Well, my Sausage actually – and Steak and Sushi and anything from Sainsbury's.

Best dance moment?

I think it might have been recently at an end-of-conference disco. One of the girls from the event company was keen on salsa. I told her about Succeeder Salsa, so we did our thing on the dance floor but it wasn't easy to 'Hi-Ho Silver Lining'. Everyone was looking on in amazement. A project manager whose girlfriend it was tried to join in but ended up getting in my way. His trailing arm gave me a cut lip so we called it a day.

Wicked-est holiday?

Every year I go to Norway. I was in Kristiansund. I saw someone who looked like Morton Harket, the former lead singer of A-Ha. We chatted for an hour and a half. He was very keen to find out about Succeederology and promised he would come on our next Succeeder Weekend. I did get his autograph (and gave him mine, of course!) but I'm still not sure it was actually Morton. As a joke, I did say, 'Take on Me' – as your business coach. Actually it wasn't meant as a joke but he laughed.

Journey (The)

> *Hey, Mr Travelin' Man,*
> *The Journey is takin' you who-knows-where.*
> *Life is a Circle,*

But maybe you're a peg that's square.

Tamma Chookworth, from 'Journey Begins with a J', *Songs for Succeeders*, **Vol. 2 (lyrics reproduced by kind permission)**

Life is a journey, isn't it? So is business. It's not a destination. Sometimes it's not the arriving that matters but the taking part. Every BUZZNESS WARRIOR is on her or his Hero's Business Journey (HBJ) in search of spiritual and commercial enlightenment. As my old friends the Buddhists say, even a journey of a thousand steps might only be a mile but at least you've saved the taxi fare.

The SUCCEEDER has many roles to play along the HBJ. Yes, there's the WARRIOR, but as the path unfolds there are others as well, based on the types of character found in folklore and fairly tales. So I have created the Mythology of Motivitalising to help you along the Journey.

Archetypes of Achievement

Archetype	Archetypal Utterance
Warrior	'I'm going to sort this once and for all!'
Innocent	'Didn't you get that email I sent?'
Orphan	'Um, I don't seem to be in the loop.'
Care-Giver	'Sharon, shall we have a coffee to discuss the new reporting structure?'
Seeker	'I'm going to surf the net and find out a bit more about ergonomic office furniture.'
Lover	'I think we all need to calm down a bit and have a meeting.'
Destroyer	'Frankly, the old kettle has given up the ghost. Let's get rid.'
Creator	'I've formed a subcommittee to look at the options for the Christmas party.'

Sage	'OK, it did go horribly wrong, but what can we learn going forward?'
Jester	'I've put that photo of Phil in his shorts at the conference as his screensaver!'
Magician	'I've called in an outside consultant, from Succeeder Solutions.'

Lake of Leadership

A place where many have swum and many have sunk. Sometimes it can be a lonely place. You're stuck far from the bank without a paddle, with the ducks quacking all around you. Remember what Haircut 100 said (in their song 'Love Plus One')?

Where does it go from here?
Is it down to the lake I fear?

I'm sure that's a feeling shared by many people in near-leadership positions.

See also RIVER OF RAGE.

Laptop

Something that sits on the lap and makes work life much easier to bear. Not to be confused with a PA. It's great to be able to work on the move. Wherever I am, I can continue writing. Those are my Three Rs – Writing, Writing and Writing. No wonder I've managed to publish so many books (*see* Appendices for full list of titles). For example, I am at the home of a coachee now and she's just making dinner so I can spend a few moments continuing with my work. Ah, she's brought some crisps out now, so I'd better stop typing, otherwise I'll put mucky fingers on the keyboard ... See you later!

Ooops! I was all ready to get some more words down before giving good meeting at the Luton Hilton North with a prospective client (a not-for-profit enterprise that is seeking to put the fun back in Stevenage) when I realised that I had left my laptop at my coachee's house this morning. Luckily she was able to drop it back at the office on her way to work at the Luton Nail Salon and the security guard handed it on to me this afternoon. Let's hope he wasn't peeking at my Powerpoint slides on SUCCEEDEROLOGY! On second thoughts, it might not have been so bad if he had. He's got an attitude which ill behoves one in the service sector.

Law of Unintended Consequences

'Whenever a change is effected, consequences will follow, some unintended, some intended. If you're not careful there will be more unintended ones than intended ones.'

L. Vaughan Spencer

Remember this, change agents and PDB professionals! You think you could be bringing in great change, but many will see it as an attack on their fiefdom or their very self, both of which may actually be the case.

Who could have foreseen that the local dry-cleaner's would lose half its customers simply because we rebranded it as 'Dirt Dancing'?

Who would have thought that a senior executive from a stationery supply company who came on my anger management course would end up as a nun?

Who would have thought that sending my wife to spy on a Frankie B course would have led to her eventually running off with him?

Lawyernoia

Fear of lawyers. Certainly I have developed a great fear of my ex-wife's representatives. But a lawyer can be a great friend in BUZZNESS, helping with HEALTH AND SAFETY legislation, terms of employment and libel suits when someone has misunderstood a light-hearted joke you've made in the *Dunstable Gazette*.

Lead

1. The thing that leaders do.
2. Also a term in SALES, as in 'I'm following a lead' or 'lead generation'. A lead is an unsuspecting person whose phone number you've got.
3. Something you put on dogs to keep them from running away. Some sales reps do this with their customers, but it may not work in all circumstances.

So how do you get a phone number when you meet a possible lead?

☆ Ask for it.

☆ Ask for it again.

☆ Plead for it.

☆ Look it up in the phone book.

☆ Ask someone else who knows it.

☆ Pinch their mobile phone, ring yourself and note the caller's number.

Leadership

As in 'Lack of …', 'Crisis in …', 'Need for strong …' and Leadership Vacuum. So, leadership is difficult to pinpoint but its absence is very apparent. Leadership is about leading. There is much talk of late of the Servant-Leader. He (or she!) sets out to serve others and help them to grow. That's all very well, but it doesn't go far enough. Here are some other leadership archetypes we have observed, the Seven Ls:

Absent-Leader – doesn't get in the way
Auntie-Leader – cuddles and makes tea
Bully-Leader – shouts and shoves
Chum-Leader – everyone's friend
Dude-Leader – is so cool you can't help following
Lost-Leader – is so bad that everyone steps up to the
  plate and gets on with things anyway (similar to
  Leader-as-Laughing-Stock)
Louche-Leader – leads by buying drinks

It can be useful to study great leaders, such as:

Braveheart
Top Cat
Darth Vader
David Beckham
Trevor MacDonald
Rambo
Captain Kirk (of *Star Trek*)
Sir Alan Sugar
Natasha Kaplinsky
Queen Elizabeth the Queen Mother (who started the
  Queen Mother Theatre in Hitchin)

What do each of them have in common? Nerves of steel, true

grit, HOCUS-FOCUS and, very importantly, Chill-Outness. A great leader knows when to stand down his troops and take them ten-pin bowling. Metaphorically speaking, there are Large Leaders and Little Leaders. Are you Little or Large? After interviewing a sample (more than one) of leaders, here's what we found characterised each.

Large Leadership	Little Leadership
Being a role model	Hiding
Making decisions	Making paper aeroplanes
Shouting (when necessary)	Shouting (too much)

> ### *A Lyric for Leadership*
> *Are you tough enough*
> *To take the smooth with the rough?*
> *Can you the dragon rebuff?*
> *You may puff and huff*
> *And use your powder puff*
> *But soon they'll call your bluff.*
> *You may be left in the buff*
> *If you ain't tough enough.*

Tamma Chookworth, *Songs for Leaders (Small to Medium Enterprises)*

(lyrics reproduced by kind permission)

See also MANAGEMENT and LIPSTICK LEADERSHIP.

Learning

As in Learning and Development (L&D if you like – not to be confused with Luton and Dunstable!). These two words are very close to my heart. In fact, they're tattooed near my left nipple. I yearn to learn. Yes, even someone at my level in the heady world of L&D has some things to learn!

A recent government review rightly addressed the

problem of children emerging from school without the skills actually needed in the workplace. What are these 'soft' yet so very hard skills? Children may learn math and English at school but they don't necessarily get any instruction in real BUZZNESS skills, such as:

> How to defend your space in an open-plan office (e.g. by building walls of lever arch files).
>
> How to behave at the Christmas party.
>
> How to make sure the boss gives you credit when things go well and blames others when things go badly.

The L. Vaughan Spencer Foundation is a Learning Organisation (and an earning one – we don't get involved in all that sub-prime malarkey!). In fact, I insist that all my employees and associates take part in my development workshops, at their own expense. It's the only way to ensure they make the most of them. Our courses are not delivered in the usual way either. Apart from E-LEARNING, there's T-Learning, where students learn while in the toilet. We find it highly effective, especially for Sales Techniques.

But, of course, the only way to really learn is on the job, under the guidance of a great leader. The watchword is Coach. It's no coincidence that that also means a big vehicle taking people on a journey of discovery to an exciting destination! Is yours roadworthy? Are you carrying excess baggage? Is there a Learn-o-meter fitted? Have you planned enough comfort stops?

Legacy

'The mess left behind by the last CEO,' says my friend Frederick. Or it is something left in a will. Though there won't be much in mine for a while, thanks to the machinations of my ex-wife's lawyer. Yet the legacy I leave behind will be something amazing … a world full of MOTIVITALITY, with individuals and teams and organisations fully Succeederised, HOCUS-FOCUSED on GOALS. I like to think of myself being spoken of in the same breath as the great humanitarians of our age – Martin Luther King, Nelson Mandela, Donald Trump and John Craven. But perhaps my legacy will be something straightforward – simply the word SUCCEEDER, symbolising a world where there will be no SUCCESS-O-PHOBES, everyone will embrace their natural-born right to SUCCEEEDINESS© and BUZZNESS will look quite different.

If you were dead, would anyone really care? A great exercise is 'Write Your Own Eulogy'. Here are some notes for mine (to be read by Frankie B):

'We shall never see his like again. L. Vaughan Spencer made a difference. He was the difference. He gave his all. He changed lives. Few people realised how much he did for charity for example, starting the L. Vaughan Spencer International Conflict Resolution Center. He donated a day of his coaching skills free to Relate (the relationship guidance people) and was very open about what went wrong in his first marriage; why they didn't ask him back is a mystery. Wasn't it great that the Succeederthon© he organised in 2013 raised a hundred million pounds for Businesspeople in Need? He created the L. Vaughan Spencer Foundation, a charitable organisation that helps losers and non-achievers, as well as Succeeder Solutions, a hands-on consultancy alongside Succeeder Lab, its research arm and the think tank the Succeeder Institute, which lobbied the government to create the Buzzness Taskforce, headed by Mary Queen of Shops. This was a

man of letters, a man of passion, a man of action. He
wouldn't want us to spend the whole of the month
mourning him. He would exhort us to return to our hot
desk, to Give Even Better Meeting, to become great Room
Workers. In fact, this funeral is a Prime Networking
opportunity, with all the top people from the Succeeder
Triangle gathered here. Get your Buzzness Cards
a-buzzing! Of course, L-Vo has been buried with his
remaining cards. So continue his great work and keep on
giving 166 per cent more than the Max!'

Levels of Language

What we say can be what we mean. Train yourself and your
staff (especially call centre workers) to aim for the top
level.

Low Level	On the Level	Top Level
OK	Yes	You betcha
Deal with	Sort out	Take it to the Max!
Content	Happy	Bursting with joy
I will try	I can	I'm gonna stop at nothing till you become an advocate for our brand!
Goodbye	Thank you for calling	I'm like so totally into you!

Life-Changer

Frankie B. Yeah, right.

Lipstick Leadership

The great question hanging over all female leaders: Can you Look Great *and* Lead Great? Of course you can! Look at three great Lady Leaders – The Queen, Margaret Thatcher and Natasha Kaplinsky. We are in world of post-CHAPITALISM! Welcome to CHICK-ITALISM. You can be a Buzzness Babe or a Power Poppet. To encourage women in business, we have created the Miss Motivitality competition. It's open to anyone in the SUCCEEDER TRIANGLE. Forget catwalks, swimsuits and evening gowns, this is about enterprise. Just think the Three Fs – Femininity, Finance and Fashion. Each lady must come and deliver a speech on 'A Business Challenge Facing the Herts and Beds Conurbation'. The judges (the manageress of the Luton Nail Salon, Les Goodhall and my good self) will be looking for poise and commercial acumen. It's all to kick off our new initiative, Succeeder Sistas, which will make sure that the boardrooms of Luton, Stevenage, Watford and satellite areas are fully representative of the fairer sex. The prize is a bottle of sparkling wine and half an hour's coaching from yours truly. Succeeder Sistas! Join in the L-VOLUTION! But let's keep the divine secrets of the Yo-Yo Sistahood! So as not to be seen to be sexist, we are also holding a Mr Motivitality competition (*see* MANLINESS).

Lunch

Vital in today's fast-moving business environment (FMBE). Professor Trankin of the Jimmy Connors Institute of Business found that 83 per cent of people eat lunch in the middle of the day.

There are two sorts: the Business Lunch, held over ninety minutes, and the Rushed Solitary Lunch (RSL), held over seventeen minutes or less (timed from leaving office chair, through journey to outsourced sandwich dispensary to returning and eating 'al desko'). Lunch needs to be much more productive. For example, it was over lunch that Ned agreed to publish this book. Research from the Succeeder Lab shows that 63 per cent of Buzzness Bonds are forged over lunch. What about the remaining 37 per cent? When or where else is true commercial connectedness consummated? According to Professor Trankin, it's as follows:

Phone 11%
Email 9%
In the car park 8%
Sauna 0.1%
Other (hairdresser's, casinos, fight clubs) 8.9%

source: Succeeder Institute 2004

Luton Futon

Luton's leading futon shop – where 'A Good Night's Sleep Really Does Come Cheap'. They sponsor *The Succeeder Hour*. They supplied (as part of the sponsorship!) a futon which I use in my office. When I want to GIVE GOOD MEETING, or if I've been CREATIVISING particularly hard, or it's a phone-coach session that requires real HOCUS-FOCUS, the futon feels the force. I can do some great thinking lying on it (often while listening to *Steve Wright in the Afternoon*), as Nikki now understands. She used to burst in and think I was sleeping. Now she knows better. I hope she will return.

Luton Lingo

See L-VOCABULARY.

L. Vaughan Spencer Foundation

A social enterprise dedicated to making the world a better place. One of the jewels in our crown is the L. Vaughan Spencer International Conflict Resolution Center, already making quite a noise in the Herts & Beds area.

Trustees: Veronica Spencer, Les Goodhall, Mandy, Professor Krench, the Mayor of South Mimms and Nick Owen's brother.

L-Vo

Yours truly: the President of the Republic of Success. Are you ready to become a citizen?

L-Vocabulary

Sometimes known as LUTON LINGO.

A new way of seeing the world, expressed through language. Certain words in English don't exist in L-Vocab (doubt, problem, cabbage) and vice versa (MOTIVITALITY, SUCCEEDEROLOGY, BUZZNESS).

L-Vocation

Remember the watchword of career advice – 'Vocation, vocation, vocation.' Well, your L-Vocation is your real inner vocation, not the one you thought was yours when you were at school (astronaut, fire-fighter, ice-cream man) but your real one (life coach, reality show participant, CEO).

L-Volution

The revolution that is occurring in the PDB world. If Paul McKenna is the Fidel Castro of Change, then I am the Che

Guevara! Che's mission was to create something new: Socialist Man. I am creating SUCCEEDER Man (and Woman). Check out my book *The BMX Diaries*. As a youngster, I cycled around the highways and byways of Surrey in search of enlightenment with my friend Steve. He went into office partitioning but the trip radicalised me. Without a doubt. I could no longer simply walk by if I saw unfulfilled potentiality not being fulfilled.

> *Join the L-Volution!*
> *It's high-resolution*
> *And good for your constitution!*

Make Your Face Fit©

This is an easy-to-follow daily SUCCEEDER facial workout routine which makes your face more powerful and ensures that you won't need plastic surgery. Try it now. To make things simpler, I have nicknamed each movement in honour of a newsreader or TV personality as a point of concentration, so that when stretching you can really focus on that particular part of the face:

Move lip up and down – raise and lift (*Huw Edwards*).

Eyes wide open and shut (*Evan Davis*).

Roll from the shoulders (*George Alagiah*).

Eyebrows – up and down (*Emily Maitlis*).

Keep eyes still but keep jaw going for a long time (*Garth Crooks*).

Best not to do these in a meeting – unless the other participants are doing the same (e.g. if it's been pre-agreed as a MEET-ERCISE session). But if you keep exercising your face there'll be no need for any injections in your forehead! Keep Thinking Outside the Botox!

Management

Yes, it's the question that is gripping the nation right now. What is the difference between Management and Leadership? Management is about doing and Leadership is about being.

Management Is What I Do
Leadership Is What I Be!

Management	Leadership
Do	Be
Because	Why?
Help	Love
Looking	Envisioning
Celine Dion	Kylie
Alan Titchmarsh	Sir Alan Sugar
Frankie B	L-Vo

Manliness

Manliness is next to godliness; and sometimes manliness is a bit too far from cleanliness. Metrosexualism is one thing but, thanks to me, men are discovering the NEW VIRILITY, which is all about traditional virile values in a modern setting. The Men-aissance is sweeping through the workplace. We must become fully New Men – fully New and as Manly as we can manage. Think of Sir Alan Hansen – he's Scottish, he played football *and* he shops at Morrisons. It's time such men retook the citadel of the Men-tropolis from the skewed versions of the Jeremys Clarkson and Paxman. As part of our drive we have introduced the Mr Motivitality competition. Contestants must show they have not only financial muscle and a tight bottom line, but also a water-tight skincare regime to counteract crow's feet and sagging of the lower face in a downturn.

See also MEN.

Marketing

Vital in today's fast-moving business environment (FMBE), especially as we head towards the 22ND CENTURY. We are all marketers now. I get very angry when a company tells me about their marketing department. *Every* department should be in the business of marketing! If your job is to clean the washrooms that's as much about marketing as choosing logos, posters or ad campaigns, because the customer will actually remember a dirty toilet. So that's why I get the whole 'marketing' team to go and scrub the lavatory floor as the first exercise in our CREATIVISING Workshop. Remember, Marketing is BATTY:

> ### *Branding and*
> ### *Advertising*
> ### *Targeted*
> ### *To*
> ### *You*

For example, why did you buy this book rather than a longer and more expensive one by Frankie B?

1. You were desperate.
2. Someone told you what a great book this is.
3. You saw me on the front cover and thought, 'Here's a man who can help me.'

If the answer was (1), are you as desperate as you were before? If so, keep reading, but it's up to you to sort yourself out. Or to get in touch and ask for a one-on-one. Please send photo.

If the answer was (2), now you can pass on the good news

too. Remember word of mouth (WOM) is the best form of marketing. Become a WOM-BAT now!

If the answer was (3), why not take another look? Don't resist the urge to buy another.

What about marketing *you*? You are CEO of Brand You. Do you have a Plan? What are you doing for Promotion (CLOTHES, HAIR, MOISTURISER, BUZZNESS CARD)? And, most importantly, have you decided what your Product is? Maybe it's time for some Motivitalising Market Research. The best I heard was asking people, 'What company would you miss if it went out of business?' Would it make any difference if *you* were no longer available? Are you up to scratch or are you in need of a REBRAND?

See also SLOGAN.

Max

Make the most of … as in 'Max Your Life', 'Max Your MOTIVITALITY' or 'Max the Buffet, dude, it's $8.99 for All-You-Can-Eat', which is often what I do during the lunch break at conferences. Luckily, as I follow the ALPHABET DIET, I can eat as much lunch as I like because it begins with an L.

MBA

I gained my MBA at San Diego's Jimmy Connors Institute of Business one weekend. Recently, I read an article about MBA programmes being too macho, too much of a throwback to CHAPITALISM. Well, what do you expect from something called a *Master* of Business Administration? I did check out the modules on one course and I could see their point:

Thrusting into the Future
Planting the Seed of Growth

My Spreadsheet's Bigger Than Yours

I am an executive coach to lots of business ladies and I'm rolling out a much more female-friendly executive course, with modules such as:

Does My Bottom Line Look Big in This?

Crying as a Negotiating Tactic

I Don't Want Answers – I Just Need to Be Listened to

Meaningfulness

There's lots of talk these days about the Meaningful workplace. Is yours? Or is it Meaningless – or just De-Meaning? What does your work mean? *What on earth are you doing?* It's up to us in the Success Community to make sure that people find meaning in their work, even if they hate their work and all their colleagues.

Meaningfulness is about more than job satisfaction. It's about making the workplace reflect your values and fulfil your hopes and dreams, which could be tricky if you find yourself photocopying requisites for anti-personnel landmines. The SUCCEEDER only does work which accords with his or her values. For example, I have a strict rule: I work only with firms that pay me.

Work should be about expressing yourself and allowing you to be creative – unless you are an accountant.

Quiz: Is Your Workplace Meaningful?

How do you feel when you go into work on a Monday?

(a) Oh no – not another week.

(b) I can't wait till the weekend, when I can do what I really want.

(c) Can I call in sick again?

(d) Hooray – the beginning of another week in which I
will feel even more empowered and fully alive.

Meaningfulness is vital in the WAR ON TALENT. We must
create Meaningful Engagement to retain people, unless they
aren't very good, in which case we should let them go and
find Meaning at the JobCentre. Where do we get Meaningfulness from outside our jobs? From our children. Last week I
had employees' children come in and provide Meaning by
shifting some filing cabinets and agreeing next year's budget.
Or maybe Meaning comes from hobbies. So integrate your
hobby and your job! One of my clients was keen on stamp
collecting. He was CEO of a major PLC but, thanks to me, he
isn't any more. Now he has plenty more time for his philately
between shifts as a postman!

How do you create Meaningfulness? Think of the Three
Rs – Relationship, Respect, Relevance. Now make sure that
you can answer these questions:

Relevance: Is there any point in what I'm doing?

Respect: Does everyone think I'm an idiot?

Relationship: Why is nobody talking to me?

What else are employees seeking? Here are some
pointers:

Three Cs: Creativity, Challenge and Company Car.

Three Ps: Purpose, Personal Development and Parking
Place (actually, that's four … Even more meaningful!)

The Meaningful Organisation is one where a Monday
looks like a Friday at other places. Not because everyone
goes home after lunch or spends it in the pub. No, it's that

If your answer was (d), then you have meaningfulness. Otherwise you
don't and you need to go and find some.

buzz of excitement as you know you are getting your teeth into something really Meaningful – like hunting some up-to-the-minute supply chain software or allocating desks in the new open-plan office.

Meaningful Space (M-Space)

A special place that has real spiritual resonance where Deep Dialogue can occur and people can leave motorcycle crash helmets and unwashed coffee cups and read old copies of *Hello!* magazine. I find that it also develops a sense of teamwork – along with an indefinable smell. It can be a haven for MOTIVITALISING MEDITATION.

Me-dership

Vital in today's fast-moving business environment (FMBE). Who is the first person you have to lead? Yourself! So start with You. Do you do as you ask yourself? Do you give yourself good FEEDBACK? Do you really appreciate yourself? Do you give yourself a hug? Do you give yourself an honest APPRAISAL – and do you take your own advice? Quite probably not! Allow yourself to make mistakes. But then don't allow yourself to make the same ones again.

It's time for Self-LEADERSHIP – Me-dership. I have to lead me. I have to make sure I am keeping up. I have to set a good example to myself and then be sure to follow it. I have to tell me to pull my socks up now and then, or take myself to one side to give myself a good talking to, a frank ME-ON-ME. And there are times when I just need to enjoy me, give me a pat on my back. Remember, in Me-dership:

If You Can't Lead Yourself You Can't Lead Anyone Else!

Meet-ercise

Meetings can be bad for the SUCCEEDER's health. It's not good to sit still for too long, eating biscuits sitting in non-ergonomic chairs around a table of laptops and lapdogs. Keep active while talking. Keep the body engaged as well as the mind. Why not hold the meeting in the gym? Or in the sauna? Or running round the park? Or while having a bout of SUCCEE-DO, the Martial Art of MOTIVITALITY? Why not hold the meeting while doing Pilates or yoga (or YO-YOGA if it's a negotiation)? Or tennis?

Work a Work-out into Your Work!

It's best if this is agreed in advance. It's no good turning up to a meeting in jogging pants if the other parties are in their normal work outfits, as I did once with the Bishop of St Albans, though that SUCCEE-DO victory was one of my finest.

Meeting-itis

A dangerous disease which afflicts so many individuals and organisations. They cannot do anything without having a meeting about it. And even then they don't do anything except schedule another meeting. I take radical action – by renaming Meeting Rooms as:

>Waste-of-Time Rooms
>
>Action Rooms
>
>No-More-Elephants-in-the-Room Rooms

With one company, I arranged a meeting to discuss the endemic Meeting-itis. Nobody turned up, so it had clearly worked.

See also GIVE GOOD MEETING.

Meeting Motivator

I often go into organisations simply to reinvigorate their meetings – to teach them how to GIVE GOOD MEETING. With one firm, I made them sit in silence for thirty minutes. Judging by the amount of noise they made when they came out, they all emerged with more energy and HOCUS-FOCUS than from any previous meeting.

'L-Vo has created a step-change in the way we run meetings. His radical approach has definitely had an effect on the bottom line of at least 3 per cent. He's even had input into when the coffee trolley comes in, who drives it and the things on it. He takes my breath away.'

Oswal Ankermann, CIO International E-Chunking, Inc.

'Thanks to L-Vo, we no longer have any meetings. We just have Multi-Person Meaningful Interfaces. He has saved us well over a thousand pounds, which is good, since his fee was a bit more than we expected. We have had to have several meetings to sort it out.'

Henrietta Banfield, MD, 'Find Your Fun in Stevenage'

Meetings

Before arranging one, the SUCCEEDER takes some time to answer the following questions:

> Do we really need this meeting?
> Do I really need to be there?
> Does *he* really need to be there? And her? And him?
> Could I do the meeting with just one other person?
> Can we do it standing up?
> Do we really need to hire a meeting room and a tray of coffee and tiny pastries?

Could I do it on my own at my house?

Can we put a time-limit on it?

How about a quarter of an hour?

Recent research by Professor Krench of Succeeder Lab says that most meetings tend to have only eleven minutes that are actually productive. Here's how things broke down for a typical meeting:

Predicted length: 1 hour

Actual length: 1 hour 13 minutes (73 minutes)

Productive time: 11 minutes

Getting started (waiting for late-comers, for early-comers to go away and come back again, or for mid-comers to 'just finish this call/email/game of office quoits, it won't take long'): 6 minutes

Clarifying why some people are there and some aren't: 3 minutes

Distributing drinks and nibbles: 3 minutes

Sorting out when the next meeting will be: 4 minutes

Going over the same ground as last time: 16 minutes

Listening to people justifying their past actions: 9 minutes

Irrelevant points being raised to blame others or score points: 11 minutes

Repeating a point already made because someone wasn't listening: 4 minutes

Sorting out actions for next meeting: 5 minutes

Flirting: 1 minute (depending on the personnel involved. This can rise to the full 73 minutes, as this activity can be achieved even during all the others)

Average percentage of actions completed since previous meeting: 39%

Average number of reasons given per action why said
    action wasn't completed: 2.3

And here are some unusual stats that might be worth
bearing in mind next time you're booking a meeting room
and accompanying tea/coffee:

Per Thousand Meetings

Average number of deaths: 3.0

Average number of births: 1.0

Average number of people not realising that they are in
    the wrong meeting: 96

Average number of people wishing that they were in the
    wrong meeting: 583

Average number of meetings hit by lightning: 1.0

Number of meetings where a death, a birth *and*
    lightning have occurred: 0.1 (That was a bad day at
    Luton Clairvoyants!)

Men

Vital in yesterday's business environment (YBE) but not in
today's fast-moving business environment (FMBE). CHICK-
ITALISM don't need the dudes! Men are removed from their
traditional role of hunter-gatherer. Men are shopping, moisturising and wearing sarongs, while women are wearing
trousers and shouting and running most big corporations.
NEW VIRILITY is about being more WARRIOR-like yet more MOIS-
TURISER-aware – both of which enhance BUZZNESS – which is
the Ultimate Goal. Women are better evolved at what is really
required in modern business:

Noticing what you are wearing

Remembering what you did wrong in the past

Arranging food from the buffet on a plate neatly (they
rarely 'Max the Buffet'!)

Men's traditional skills, such as

Standing in front of a smoking barbecue

Getting things down from the loft

Standing in groups on pavements outside pubs,
muttering a few syllables and laughing uproariously

can only take them so far in BUZZNESS.

Mentor

What's the difference between a COACH and a mentor? Well, a
mentor may work in the same company or sector and so
understand the particular issues facing the mentee. A coach
hasn't got the faintest. But mentoring can go bad. The relationship may translate into overdependence or even hero-
worship. I fear this may be happening with Liam and myself.
Or there's the 'Black Halo' effect: if either mentor or mentee
makes a hash of things, the other is tarnished. Or the mentor
may nick ideas from the mentee. And either could spread
malicious gossip about the other (thus becoming a Tor-
Mentor! Feel free to use this joke.) So it's much better to
have a coach from outside your sector. We can supply you
with one. Me, for instance. Glancing at my wall-chart, I see
Tuesday morning, Thursday afternoon and Friday (any time
till 5 p.m.) are free at the moment. Please send photo.

Me-on-Me

A Self-interface, a 'one-on-the-same-one', a time for Self-
LEADERSHIP. I find these invaluable.

See also ME-DERSHIP.

Merger

Where two companies (both large) join to become one company (small, eventually), says my friend Frederick. He's obviously never experienced a Motivitalised Merger. That's where I spend months with each company, dealing with the pain and insecurity, letting the tears flow, running through role-plays, imagining the worst, so that the reality isn't quite so bad when it arrives. And the people who are let go can then come to me for some SUCCEEDER coaching.

Mission Statement

A bold statement of an organisation's values and purpose. For us it is simply: To Bring Succeediness to Where It Wasn't Before

Many of the companies I work with don't have one as aspirational as this. Here are some examples:

Nice Buns Bakery
To bake beautiful buns

Luton Nuclear Enterprises
To fully engage in sustainable growth while not upsetting people

Hitchin Crematorium
To create solutions to issue-based solution-free zones

Bucks & Beds Police
To arrest as many people as possible

Professor Krench has done some research recently and found that the biggest single factor influencing whether people are high-flyers has nothing to do with the LEADERSHIP style of their immediate superior, but everything to do with the length of the Mission Statement of the organisation. The longer it is, the more likely they are to stay. So we have changed the ones above to make them much more motivitalising:

Nice Buns Bakery
To create a fully synergised operation that respects the local environment and brings bread-based products to as wide an audience as possible while respecting each and every one of our employees and giving them one of those white hats that bakers wear

Luton Nuclear Enterprises
To become the most creative energy organisation in the Luton area while paying the utmost respect to the wealth of local history and treating every individual as we would like to be treated ourselves

Hitchin Crematorium
To become a global brand leader in the sensitive treatment of death and all aspects of bereavement and leave an indelible mark on the people of Hitchin and those who die near it

Bucks & Beds Police
To arrest as many people as possible … and complete the paperwork.

Moisturiser

Vital in today's fast-moving business environment (FMBE). Traditional management models (especially those created by men) don't take into account how important skincare is to business success. The SUCCEEDER is in touch with his or her inner WARRIOR but understands the importance of dermatological hydration. This is where many middle managers slip up. One of my business mentors – a Medicine Man in Alpacqua Wacqua in French Canada – used to say, 'Man with dry face no win big deal. Pass the Boots Number 7.' A dry face is not a Succeedy face – it won't win new business.

Moisturiser and Men

Research shows that men are 16 per cent thicker-skinned than women. Their skin is oilier, drier and more easily hydrated, so it's even more important for us to moisturise. Women have been moisturising for a thousand years. We've been doing it for twenty. We've got a lot of catching up to do. So first find a role model … Jon Snow, Bill Clinton and Sir Alan Hansen are all famously in the vanguard of Succeeder Skincare (Sir Alan gets his at Morrisons). Don't underestimate what can be achieved. For example, a great concealer could cover up your ugly bits. Professor Krench conducted a survey that showed nice skin and clothes are more attractive to ladies than a car – I bet he enjoyed that research!

Have you tried our BOY-STURISER or, if you're over forty-five and getting saggy and baggy, Mensturiser. Some men worry that moisturising and masculinity are incompatible. Phooey! There is a line to be drawn, though. For the SUCCEEDER, skincare should be fully aligned with business objectives. If you are spending more time in the bathroom than in the boardroom you have gone too far. Aim to be constantly in front of the competition – not constantly in front of the mirror.

There's more about our skincare and shaving products in the Appendices.

Moti-Mantra

A motivational mantra. Something you say to yourself a lot to HOCUS-FOCUS on your GOALS. It helps the I-Brain to empty itself of all but motivational thoughts. You can create your own, but here are a few that might get you started:

>   I Am Succeedy (× 2)
>   I Will Always Love Myself
>   I Am Myself and Nobody Else
>   Motivitality Overcomes Obstacles (shortened to MOO –
>   useful for intoning on difficult days)

Moti-Music

The Soundtrack of Success. Motivitalising Music is goal-oriented and uplifting. For example, 'Promised You a Miracle' by Simple Minds is perfect for IN-CAR MOTIVITALISING on the way to a difficult sales call. To help you achieve maximum HOCUS-FOCUS I have suggested some particularly relevant songs for certain BUZZNESS moments (*see* Appendices). Thanks to one of Liam's friends (whom I have nicknamed Monsieur Moti-Mixer) a Moti-Mix, 'mashing up' well-known songs with some rapping by yours truly, should be available next year, with tracks like:

>   'We Are Succeedy' (to Sister Sledge's 'We Are Family')
>   'Succeeder' (to the tune of 'Tequila')
>   'Yes Sir I'm Succeedy' (to Baccara's 'Yes Sir I Can
>   Boogie')

Some will be downloadable as ringtones. Liam's working on it. *See* Appendices for more.

Motivation

So 20th century. Without a doubt; a shadow of a doubt. I have moved beyond that (*see* MOTIVITALITY), yet I still get mentioned in the same breath as the current lame crop of charlatans – the so-called YBM (Young British Motivators) and the oh-so-yawn-worthy poster boys of 'nu-Motivation'.

Moti-Verse

The SUCCEEDER is a poet-WARRIOR in the classical sense. A Moti-Verse gets her (or him) HOCUS-FOCUSed on the battle ahead; it's a lyrical weapon in the motivator's armoury. Plain English is well and good in its place. The words of company reports can be really uplifting and exciting, but they don't always truly nourish us. The language of LEADERSHIP takes us beyond mere sentences into the realm of ethnopoetic reality, I read somewhere. That's where I come in. You may have heard of the rap star 50 Cent. Well, I am L-Vo, the 50 Cent for the White Collar Dollar. I find that rap poetry can hit the places that mere prose cannot reach.

Here's a SUCCEEDER stanza to encourage you.

Are you ready to be great?
Then it's time to motivate.
I am the Shark of the Chakra.
I am the fluid druid not from Clwyd.
I inflame the vortex of your cortex.
I can break your mould
And turn base metal into gold.
I bless the entity which is your identity.
It's time to leave the fold,
So be bold and cross the threshold!

Motivitalising Meditation (Moti-Meditation)

Old-fashioned meditation is too difficult, because you have to think of nothing and chant and do it for a long time in a quiet place. You can do Moti-Meditation at your desk, in the car or near a radiator. Try some now. Concentrate on my picture on the front cover of this book. See the SUCCEEDER FINGERS I am holding up? The thumb and forefinger make an L: for Life, Love or Lunch – your choice. Make that L-shape with both your hands and point at your ears and very quietly hum 'OM, OM, OM' – which stands for Organisational Meaningfulness. Amazing, isn't it? Hasn't it transformed a dull day into a Dream Day! Often I use this in phone coaching, and the client may spend up to fifty minutes intoning 'OM', while I can get on with some Sudoku or sipping a meaningful glass of Chardonnay.

Motivitality

Motivation synergised with Vitality, twin sister of SUCCEEDEROLOGY. Succeederology is all scientific and robust. Motivitality is more female – cuddly and inner. One is steak, the other is tofu. One is mahogany, the other is cashmere. Motivitality is just one of the holistic trinity of Personal Self-Enhancement – along with Succeederology and hocus-focus. If Sir Alan Sugar is the Succeederology of PSE, then Motivitality is the bloke who sits next to him in *The Apprentice* and hocus-focus is the woman. Or to put it another way, John Noakes and Peter Purves needed the hocus-focus that was Valerie Singleton. Or if Bono and the Edge are Succeederology and Motivitality, then hocus-focus is the one who plays bass, or the one who plays drums. Whichever's the one who wears glasses.

Motivitality Check

Going beyond a reality check into Deep Due Diligence. Is this company in the Mountains of MOTIVITALITY or in the Delta of Despair? Is it a washed-out rag or a burning fire? Would people recommend it to their friends? Here are some comments from a company I worked with recently where there was Zero Motivitality:

'The Boss is an idiot (not Bruce Springsteen obviously!).'

'I nick as much as I can from the stationery cupboard. And I deliberately wait till my phone battery is low so I can nick electricity as well.'

'I wish I could get a job somewhere else, but working here counts against me.'

'I'm planning to blow up the buildings tomorrow.'

Needership

The opposite of LEADERSHIP. The act of *not* being in charge such that your team has to help you out all the time.

Net Lag

Like jet lag, which occurs when you've spent a long time in the air, this occurs when you've spent too long on the net. You find it hard to focus or to speak properly. It certainly seems to afflict Liam and those French exchange students at the internet café.

Networkee

One who is subjected to NETWORKING. He or she will be grateful for your networking skill.

Networking

Talking to people you don't like in the hope that they'll like you, says my friend Frederick. But Networking is vital in today's FMBE. The opposite is NOTWORKING – where a top chance to network is thrown away due to lack of HOCUS-FOCUS. Getting changed next to someone in the tennis club changing room? Network! It doesn't matter if you're wearing nothing apart from socks! Filling your car with petrol? Network with that other motorist or the cashier! Without networking, my career would be in tatters.

Top Tips for Networking

☆ Everybody is a potential NETWORKEE. There isn't a person who might not be useful in the future.

☆ Don't be frightened to give them your SUCCEEDER BUZZNESS CARD. Best if done in the first thirty seconds of the networking encounter. If they have been on a Succeeder course they will offer you theirs and do the SUCCEEDER GREETING. This involves the SUCCEEDER FINGERS (*see* front cover) of both hands pointing at the eyes. Enjoy the moment, a shared secret of Succeedy solidarity.

☆ Try to get their card. If necessary, ask up to twenty-three times.

☆ End the encounter with, 'I have enjoyed meeting you. I am sure we will both profit from this networking opportunity very soon. Call me any time of the day or night.'

☆ Don't be the first to break eye contact. Keep it for several minutes if needs be.

Networthy

Someone worthy of being networked. Here are some people who are Not-Networthy. Don't bother NETWORKING with:

Members of your own family
Children
Criminals (unless white collar)
Pets (unless owned by your boss)

Neuro Bureau

The place in your brain where BUZZNESS ideas come from. A bit like the Citizens' Advice Bureau but with fewer leaflets and people in the waiting room.

New Virility

We are redefining what it is to be a man in the post-post-feminist (PPF) era, moving beyond Metrosexualism to NEW VIRILITY so we can once again rejoin women at the top table of BUZZNESS. Time to discover Modern Masculinity without being a RETRO HETERO.

Quiz: Are You Ready for New Virility?

1. You are on a sunny holiday. What do you wear?
   (a) Slacks.
   (b) Sarong.
   (c) Culottes.
2. What does PDA mean to you?
   (a) Personal Digital Assistant.
   (b) Public Display of Affection.
   (c) Public Display of Ashtanga Yoga.
3. Something really, really upsetting happens. How do you react?
   (a) You keep quiet and get on with things.
   (b) You let it all out, sobbing.
   (c) You chant, then go and get a Deep-Tissue Ego Massage with Cranston.
4. What is your chosen participatory sport?
   (a) Kick-around on a Sunday morning.
   (b) Triathlon.
   (c) The Watford Race of Death.

5. What is your favourite way to eat potatoes?
   (a) Chips.
   (b) Baked.
   (c) Juiced with gingko and fennel.
6. You need to admonish your team. Do you:
   (a) Shout?
   (b) Listen?
   (c) Shout, but appropriately, with follow-on counselling?
7. You need a new cardigan. What should it be made of?
   (a) Wool-mix V-neck pullover.
   (b) Cashmere.
   (c) I use a gilet (one of those outdoor jackets without arms).
8. You are a TV personality. Are you:
   (a) Terry Wogan?
   (b) Gary Lineker?
   (c) Huw Edwards?

Mostly (a): You are part of the Old Guard of Virility.

Mostly (b): You are a Metrosexual.

Mostly (c): Well done! Welcome to the New Virility!

No

The second most important word in business (after YES). Are you prepared to say it? I have learned the Power of No. I am so busy, with speaking engagements being offered constantly almost every month, that I needed to learn to say no.

See also SUCCEEDER NO.

Learn a Good Way of Saying No!

No-Listic

The opposite of holistic. Anti-synergistic. When someone is busy looking something up on Wikipedia, while someone three desks down could tell them the answer. Or when the sales force don't use the SALES Collateral carefully prepared by the Marketing Department and just insist on asking for tickets to Wimbledon instead. Or in doubles at tennis when somebody who hasn't got a backhand plays on the wrong side of the court (mentioning no names, but Nikki's dad may be blushing if he's reading this). And it's certainly No-Listic when you want to book a top motivational speaker and don't go direct to his website (e.g. thesucceeder.com).

> *You don't have to be a mystic*
> *To know that it's best to think holistic*
> *Or you might send someone ballistic.*

Non-Achiever

The opposite of a SUCCEEDER, but one step up from a loser.

> *Are you a Succeeder or a Non-Achiever?*
> *Are you Nelson Mandela or David Mellor?*
> *Are you a guerrilla or just a form-filler?*
> *Are you Che Guevara or Palmer-Tompkinson Tara?*
> *Are you A-ha or Uh-oh?*
> *Are you bling-bling or ming-ming?*
> *Are you a Succeeder or a Non-Achiever?*

Here are the different Levels of Success:

☆ Master Succeeder
☆ Succeeders' Succeeder
☆ Succeeder
☆ Achiever

☆ Non-Achiever
☆ Loser

I am pleased to say that I have recently attained the status of Master Succeeder, awarded by the SUCCEEDER INSTITUTE in a special ceremony at the Watford Ramada Jarvis Hotel attended by the last but one Mayor of Bushey.

No-Swearing Rule

One that I try to introduce in every organisation where I work. Not always successfully, even here, thanks to Nikki, I'm afraid. Why she feels the need to swear around me, I don't know.

Notworking

Failing to capitalise when a NETWORKING opportunity presents itself. Can you think of all the times you failed to network in the past week? I bet there are plenty. Just to make you feel better, here are some of mine:

☆ *I failed to network* at Morrisons supermarket. There was a man looking for yogurt when I was. He was wearing a suit, so could easily have been in the market for a coach.

☆ *I failed to network* at the gym. There was a woman who moved my towel from one of the pushing machines. I sensed that she ran her own business. So I must remember to take BUZZNESS CARDS with me to the gym. Though my Lycra shorts don't have a pocket.

☆ *I failed to network* at 10.30 yesterday morning. Just as I was arriving at the office, someone rang us. It was a wrong number. He was looking for furniture restorers.

Only afterwards did I realise I should have said that we restore the Furniture of Life. We had a good ten minutes' chat about his sideboard. Perhaps his self-esteem needed reupholstering? Nobody's rung us since then, so I might try last-number redial and see if he likes tennis.

You see, even Master Succeeders can fall down. I hope you found that encouraging.

Write a list today of all your Notworking moments in the past week:

I failed to network at . . . .

Next time I will network.

(sign your name here) . . . .

Office Politics

The SUCCEEDER knows that there is always office politics, just as day follows night, so wise up. Remember, you must

Be Alert to Assert!

Know who you want to INFLUENCE and influence them whenever you can. Find them in the canteen, on the golf course or in their car. Go to their houses if necessary.

There are two kinds of politics: See-Through and Subtle. The former is all about figures, targets, hierarchy – the stuff that can be measured or put in a company report. Subtle Succeeder Power Plays are long-term, flexible, mutual and you won't always know they are happening. Make a Movers & Shakers Map and zero in on them. That's how I got to be such good friends with Les Goodhall.

Quiz: How Good Are You at Power Politics?

1. You want a good appraisal from your boss. Do you:
   (a) Complete all tasks given you on time?
   (b) Lend him your copy of *Hello!* magazine?
2. A colleague doesn't pull his weight. Do you:

    (a) Suggest to your boss that there's a problem that needs discussing?

    (b) Leave a dead horse on his desk?

3. The Chief Executive lives near you. Do you:

    (a) Say hello when you bump into her at the newsagents?

    (b) Conceive a child so that you can ask her to be its godmother?

But what about when things go wrong? At one organisation I worked with, they were all so busy playing politics that nobody did any work and couldn't even remember what they were supposed to be doing (it was the Department of Cheese at the Ministry for Agriculture). So we broke down barriers, through URBAN TRIBAL DRUMMING, Motivational Muffin Moments and Intimacy Interventions.

The SUCCEEDER achieves true intimacy with her or his colleagues. Not in a rude way or anything – this is something much deeper. If you know yourself you can allow others to know you. This is Deep Intimacy. Intimacy = Into-Me-See. This facilitates True Teamwork. Barriers are relaxed and Manyness can become One-ness. This worked particularly well with Abercromby District Council's refuse department.

See TEAM.

One-on-One

My favourite kind of interface.

Mostly (a): You are a See-Through Power Player.
Mostly (b): You are a Subtle Power Player.

Onside

When everyone is on your *side* rather than on your *case*.

Overload-anoia

When there's too much information. Every day we receive emails, junk mail, sights and sounds, and it's all getting too much. 'Overcoming Overload-anoia' is one of our SUCCEEDER weekend courses. Come to the Ramada Jarvis Hotel in Watford and you'll get no information. We just sit in SUC-CEEDER SILENCE for two days. Cost £45. There are optional extras – a Succeeder Salsa Session with Mandy or a walk – a guided tour through the Highways and Byways of Old Watford (both £13 extra).

In the meantime, here are a few tips:

☆ Listen to some music that has the same tempo as brain waves (baroque is good, or *Steve Wright in the Afternoon*).

☆ Manage your environment. Exclude noise, bright light or any members of the IRRITATI.

Panto Parallels

We all know that most businesses are pantomimes. Last December, I saw *Cinderella*. The story seemed so reminiscent of organisational behaviour:

Once there was a widower (*new Head of Department*) who married a proud and haughty second wife (*merged two existing departments*). She had two daughters, the Ugly Sisters (who resented the merger), who were equally haughty. By his first wife, the widower had a beautiful young daughter. The Stepmother and her daughters made Cinderella do all the housework (*dull admin stuff*).

The Prince (*Director of HR and Talent Development*) invited every maiden in the land to a ball (*Team-building Event at a Holiday Inn Express*). As the Ugly Sisters swept away to the event, Cinderella cried in despair. Her Fairy Godmother (*Organisational Change Consultant, often yours truly!*) appeared and vowed to assist Cinderella in attending the ball. She then turned Cinderella's rags into a beautiful gown (*Matalan outfit*), complete with a delicate pair of glass slippers (*bespoke Nike trainers*). She turned a pumpkin into a coach (*developed Cinderella's ideas into a top Powerpoint presentation with accompanying interactive learning exercise*).

At the ball, the entire gathering was entranced by Cinderella (*listened intently to her presentation and discussed it in depth, with Post-it notes and flip charts to capture the learnings*), especially the Prince. Cinderella only just remembered to leave as the clock struck midnight (*as the Director of HR and Talent Development questioned her further on her ideas for cross-disciplinary synergies*). She hurried out but lost one of her shoes on the steps of the palace (*car park of the Holiday Inn Express*). The Prince vowed to find the maiden to whom it belonged and marry her (*give her increased responsibilities for future intradepartmental processes*).

The Prince tried the slipper on all the maidens in the land (*conducted in-depth staff appraisals*). The stepsisters tried the shoe on (*went through psychometric testing*) in vain. Cinderella asked if she could have a go. Naturally, it fitted perfectly. Cinderella married the Prince (*became his number two, eventually succeeding him when he was promoted due to his – well actually, her – brilliant ideas for reorganising departmental processes*).

The stepsisters also married two lords (*were moved sideways into 'strategic roles' without any loss of benefits*).

How many times have we felt like saying, 'Oh no, you're not!' at a meeting, or 'He's behind you' at a conference? The main thing in any organisation is finding out who the principal boy is and what makes her tick. Not all the chorus can follow the steps and dividing your audience in two may be the only way to make them 'sing'. However, you always have a genie on hand. If you can't find a lamp to rub, just email me via thesucceeder.com.

Personality Types

It's important to know your personality type, both as a COACH and as a real person, so you can know your strengths and work on your weaknesses. For example, if you've been described as a 'resource provider' or 'completer-finisher' you might want to think about taking up a hobby or come on my course 'Why Dull Is Dynamite'.

Where are your weaknesses? As a starter, why not take my DLT ('Don't Like' Test – not Dave Lee Travis!)? Then we can begin to see where you need most work. Which of these best describes you? You can choose one or more.

I don't like … people.

I don't like … facts.

I don't like … ideas.

I don't like … pictures.

I don't like … foreigners.

I don't like … cheese.

If you said yes to all of these, you may not be suited to working in most businesses. Have you thought about becoming an insolvency practitioner?

For others, the good news is that you can change. Knowing where you are means that you will know where you used to be when you aren't there any more.

There are various personality tests on the market – Myers-Briggs, the Big 5, the Great 8 or the Terrific 12. Forget them. Succeeder Lab has developed the Succeedy Six ways to measure people.

Succeedy Six	What It means
Clothes	Have they done COLOUR THERAPY? Are they a 'brown' wearing black? Or are they fully aligned chromatically?
Moisturise	Is their skincare regime up to par? Do they cleanse and tone? Do they use pre-shave skin scrub and post-shave balm?
Hair	How's their TONG SHUI©? Can the DRAGON of failure attack through their side-parting? Do those sideburns keep them focused? Does that Bed-Head cut really suit them?
Food	Are they eating the right things? Are they following the ALPHABET DIET?
Goals	Have they got any? Have they written them down?
Everything Else	What do they seem like? Do you like them?

Of course, it's important for anyone in training to be fully armed before they go into battle. Using clever metrics based on information from the Succeedy Six, the Succeeder Lab has identified eight Personal Personality Types (PPT)©. The MOTIVATE-8 will help you identify strengths and weaknesses.*

The MOTIVATE-8

Type	Strengths	Areas for Development
Loser	Not much expected	No friends
Slacker	Doesn't overpromise	Never delivers
Slow-Coach	Methodical	Get on with it!

---

*Note for PDB professionals: it's useful to know your own.

Type	Strengths	Areas for Development
Bossy-Boots	Assertive	Gets on people's nerves
Know-All	Knows lots of things	But not as many as they think
Attention-Seeker	Everyone knows you	They wish they didn't
Worry Wort	Risk-aware	Lighten up!
Succeeder	Popular. Successful. Fab.	Promoting SUCCEEDEROLOGY©

With one company, I made them wear coloured name badges to indicate their type, so others would know how to relate to them appropriately. Unfortunately, it turned nasty. The Worry Worts didn't want to be any of the colours we had, the Attention-Seekers said their badges weren't big enough and the Slackers defaced theirs.

Phonivation©

Motivation by phone. Obviously, it's best to hold coaching sessions face-to-face, but sometimes that's just impossible if your client is on the road, or you need to get home in time for *Neighbours*. So the next best thing is the phone. With this, you can speak to one another, even when you aren't in the same room. But it does require a degree of mutual commitment. Your client must ring you. You must pick up the phone. When I do a Coach the Coach Session, people often say they find it hard to COACH at a distance. So here's what to do:

Top Tips for PDB Professionals During Phonivation©

☆ Get comfy (maybe on a COACH COUCH).

☆ Don't eat crisps – too noisy. Turkish Delight or sausages or soft fruit are OK.

☆ Have something on hand to drink (Spanish wines are good for this, though beware sparkling ones. A burp may confuse your coachee and they may interpret it as negative feedback).

☆ Say 'Mmmmm' a lot.

☆ Don't be afraid of silence. Remember the power of the SUCCEEDER SILENCE.

☆ Play back a few selected words that they say to demonstrate active listening. The following is an example that will help:

> Client: I'm not happy with the new operating structure.
>
> Coach: Not happy?
>
> Client: I feel I've been sidelined.
>
> Coach: Sidelined?
>
> Client: What do you think I should do?
>
> SILENCE
>
> Client: Hello?
>
> Coach: I was just reflecting on what you've said.
>
> Client: And …?
>
> Coach: Well, what I'm hearing you say is that you are not happy with the new operating structure because you feel sidelined.
>
> Client: That's amazing! You're exactly right.
>
> Coach: Mmmm.

Keep an eye on your watch. Remember, you're not giving your time for free! Start to wind up about ten minutes before the end-time. Use helpful phrases like:

☆ 'So, going forward …'
☆ 'Let's focus on actions.'
☆ 'That's enough, Jason, it's nearly time for *Neighbours*.'

Pin of Destiny©

Used to burst the BALLOON OF DESTINY.

P-Move (Power Move)

Every SUCCEEDER has a Power Move – a gesture that gets you right in the Zone and ready to give 166 per cent. It's a physical trigger that becomes a psychological cue for MAX MOTIVITALITY. Remember Tim Henman and his clenchy fist? P-Move helps you to P-THINK and HOCUS-FOCUS. What's yours? Experiment with some possibilities. Perhaps something featuring the elbow? Or a big kick in the air? Make sure you give yourself plenty of space – maybe in the car park rather than at your desk. Find out what others do. I use a sudden thrust of the pelvis. The Archbishop of Canterbury does a great thing with his left knee for his P-Move and Kirsty Wark's is a bit of karate chop to the floor.

Politics

My brother, Nigel, is a politician. He has been the MP for Luton (Airport South) since 2005. He sees politics as a way to change the world. I don't. That's the job of BUZZNESS. I tend to look at politics from the commercial point of view. Business is innately conservative – low taxes, light regulation, get me on a quango, give me a knighthood, yada yada. If I were Prime Minister I would think conservatism not with a small c or a big C but with a Middle C. Kidz love music – mostly in the form of ringtones and MP3s – as I have noticed when I'm trying to fight my way through the playground at Skybrook. Find someone they can tune into, think not nanny state but Supernanny State – Tough Love and Tough on the Causes of Love. Every town should have a Naughty Step, where Bad 'Uns are sent to focus on their issues and listen to chill-out music. When they're ready to apologise they must do so in a creative way – by rapping. Mash-ups are all the rage now, mixing two songs together. Take That's 'Back for Good' ('Whatever I said, whatever I did, I didn't mean it') on top of 'Sorry Seems to Be the Hardest Word' by Elton John would hit just the right note. ASBOS are too negative, so we should be rewarding good behaviour, not just punishing bad. The Prince's Trust could award 'CHASBOS', with winners receiving a text message from the man himself, saying 'U R Gr8: P/ Wales xx.'

Even though I'm not looking to be mentioned in the Queen's Birthday Honours List, I do get involved in community issues. Plans are well under way for a Live-8 style concert at the St Albans Arena, featuring local musical talent, as a way of bringing maximum pressure to bear on the council over the sequencing of traffic lights. Already confirmed for the line-up are Nigel Spencer MP, Luton Skynyrd (a local tribute to Lynyrd Skynyrd, with songs like 'Sweet Home St Albans'), Haircut 1000 (another local tribute band), the Watford Elektrik Kollektive (some young rappers from Bushey), as well as Mandy and her drama group. This is real direct action, not the fluffy talking shop that is parliamentary politics.

Presentation

Most people are terrified of giving a presentation. Recent research by the SUCCEEDER INSTITUTE has found many awful things people would do rather than give a presentation. Here they are:

What Would You Rather Do Than Give a Presentation?

Die	68%
Run naked through Woolworths	14%
Eat cardboard while cockroaches crawl over my face with Lionel Richie's 'Hello' blaring out all round	8%
Be chased by an angry lion	5%
Divorce	3%
Put my fingers in an electric socket	2%

Presenting Is Scary
But Not As Scary
As Scary Things You Can't Control!

Fear not! Help is at hand! Remember the Three Ps of Presentation:

Punctuality
Position
Powerpoint

Get there on time. Stand where they can see you. And use Powerpoint; it's great! You can get all sorts of pictures off the web that will really help. And remember, pictures are a thousand times more powerful than words. Apart from the following. These are really effective words. Use them if you can:

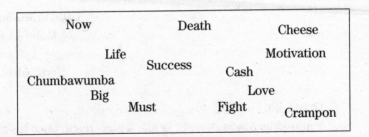

Now   Death   Cheese

Life   Motivation

Success   Cash

Chumbawumba   Love

Big   Must   Fight   Crampon

I always try to get these into any speech. They never let me down. I even managed to get them all into a eulogy for a friend recently. His family were visibly moved. One of them tried to get up and come towards me with his arms aloft, but his family kindly saw him back to his seat.

See also STRUCTURE.

P-Think (verb and noun)

Every SUCCEEDER needs to P-Think. You've heard of Positive Psychologists ('Posi-Psychos') talking about Positive Thinking. Well, this is like that but cranked up to 166 per cent. It's Positive Thinking Plus. Because it goes much further by going *beyond thinking*, P-Think encourages your brain to make new neural nodules in your cortex and your body to bolster and boost its bonus bump. It's a Positive Doing Tool (PDT), the ultimate system for lifestyle attainment. Encourage the Plus Mind. Eliminate the Minus Mind. Here's a testimonial I received from a graduate of the SUCCEEDER Weekend.

Little Fritterings
38 Miller Close
Baldock
Hertfordshire

Dear L-Vo

You told us how a thought is like a juggernaut, once it's got going it's hard to stop or change direction, and asked, 'Are you heading down the freeway of success or are you going to be run over and splattered all over the road to ruin?' Well, I didn't want to be roadkill, so I volunteered to do the next demonstration. You got me to stand in front of the Succeeder Seminar with my arm outstretched and my fist clenched, holding them as strong and as rigid as I could. Then you made me shout things like

I'm a loser.

I've got no friends.

I'm a Non-Achiever.

People point and giggle behind my back and my family
    want to disown me.

Then you leapt up and easily pushed down my arm, even though I thought I was holding it as firmly as possible.

Next you made me do it again, but this time shouting, at the top of my voice, things like:

I'm a Succeeder.

I am fully motivitalised.

With L-Vo's help I can achieve anything I want, even
    impossible things.

Then you grabbed my arm and really tried to yank it down with all your strength, and it wouldn't budge! So there you have it – total proof that there's nothing stronger than a thought! Even though my arm did hurt for the rest of the weekend and I had to sew back a button on my shirt cuff, this was a certainly profound lesson. Now I always choose to 'P-Think' and my colleagues have certainly noticed the difference – especially in murder cases. When I want to be really determined I think of you trying to force my arm down and it helps my Focus-Pocus or Hocus-Focus (can't remember which!).

Yours in grateful Succeediness
John,
Chief Superintendent,
Bucks and Beds Police

Quiet Time (aka Succeeder Silence)

Something you need. Take five minutes right now to just be quiet and do nothing. You might even put your hands on your head. Do this at work. I take five minutes every quarter of an hour. There is great power here. Certain truths can only be truly appreciated in silence. I use silence whenever possible – in coaching sessions, keynote speeches and that court case. I have found that silence is a great weapon in negotiation, coaching and a failing marriage. Have you and your team practised being silent together lately? Try it.

Some truths are beyond language.
Hey, mister, I don't want no bite
Of your reality sandwich.

Tamma Chookworth, *Songs for Succeeders*, Vol. 1
(lyrics reproduced by kind permission)

Take a Moment to Be Quiet!

Research by Professor Trankin of the Jimmy Connors Institute of Business in San Diego found that taking five minutes to be quiet increased executives' performance by 36 per cent, though not all the sample responded as they were being quiet at the time.

Rapture Capture

When I work with companies we develop some hip-hop poetry that can be a statement of their values (in total SYNERGY with their new MISSION STATEMENT), able to be rapped by all employees at important BUZZNESS moments. Here are some examples from a range of my clients:

Luton Medical Tape Systems

Medical tape, we make medical tape.
It's not just a jape
And we stay in shape!

Exhaust-o-Cure

Exhaust-o-Cure, Exhaust-o-Cure,
We'll make your car go for sure!
That is our allure.

Dunstable Abattoir

Dunstable Abattoir, Dunstable Abattoir,
To animals we say 'au revoir'.

It's not always easy to find a resonant rhyme or one that is appropriate. Asking staff is not always a good idea. It certainly wasn't at City Tankers.

Reality Check

Something that may be needed from time to time. Ask your-selves these questions:

> Is anyone buying our product?
>
> Does anyone like me?
>
> How come my wife is spending so much time getting ready for what she says is a business meeting?

Reality Will Take Care of Itself. Have You Taken a Motivitality Check?

Rebrand

Do You Need a Rebrand?

Are you sufficiently differentiated from the rest of the market? Is your 'brand' a little tired – just too 20th century? If it's time to update, here are some areas for refreshing:

Clothes	You've had that Marks & Spencer suit for six years – throw it out!
Hair	Time to lose the side-parting. <u>Men</u>: male pattern baldness creeping up your forehead? Shave it all off! <u>Women</u>: have you thought of a 'Natasha Kaplinsky'?
Moisturiser	Time to step up to twice a day. Or even thrice.
Name	Time to sex it up! I should know – see how I became L-Vo and things took off! Look at other businesses that became soaring success stories as a result of a name change: Kentucky Fried Chicken became KFC; British Telecom is now BT; Ulay became Olay; and Channel Five became Five and then it got *Neighbours*!

Here are some suggestions:

Old Name	Succeeder Styling
Lesley	L
Lionel	Lion
Valerie	Vazzer
Chris	Caramba
Sarah	Samba
Charles	Chas the Waz
Daniel	Dan the Man
Ruth	Strewth
Claire	Clazzer
Kate	K-T
Ned	Neddy C or 'N-editor' [*Ned*: This one's for you!]

See also SLOGAN.

Refrigerated Transport

In many ways, my first love in the business pantheon, even now. My heart still skips a beat when I see a Norbert Dentressangle truck, though not without a slight lump in the throat since they took over Britain's own Christian Salvesen in 2007. If you've spent hours by the M1 spotting and noting refrigerated transport vehicles, that passion never leaves you. These guys really understand pallet distribution and the logistics of chilled foods. That's why I was inspired to get my own van. At first all I had was a bucket of ice. But I soon learned to Respect the Cool Chain (as our merry song went) and acquired a refrigeration unit that kept things just right – between 2 and 5° Celsius. Our timeframes were small – we were just distributing within the Luton area and didn't have shrink-wrapping – but our customers were always more than satisfied. So it was with a heavy heart that I accepted Steve's ultimatum and let him have the van in return for 10 per cent of the business. But I wasn't so sad when it was sold years later for a fat profit. It means I can now devote myself fully to SUCCEEDEROLOGY and even have the odd afternoon off for tennis or to get my nails done.

Retro Hetero

Something of a caveman. He leaves the toilet seat up, uses ordinary soap rather than face-wash and drinks fizzy beer-like substances. He's stuck in a lay-by on the pre-metrosexual motorway and has totally missed the slip road to NEW VIRILITY. We all know one, don't we? And there are still plenty in business today. Are you one?

Boys: How to Know If You Are a Retro Hetero

Do you notice when your girlfriend's done something different with her hair?

Do you notice her earrings/her make-up/if she's in the room?

Are you more Jeremy Clarkson than Jeremy Bowen (BBC Middle East correspondent who used to have a moustache and do BBC *Breakfast*)?

If you were one of Mike and the Mechanics would you be Mike or a Mechanic?

Of course, not only men are Retro Heteros! Think of his unreconstructed female equivalent:

Girls: How to Know If You Are Retro Hetero

Do you know who Sven-Goran Eriksson is?

Do you laugh at all your partner's jokes?

Can you rewire a house?

Do you drink medium-dry white wine and have you never drunk cider and fallen down in the gutter?

Are you more Gloria Estefan or Gloria Hunniford?

Are you Posh, Sporty, Ginger, Scary or a bit of a Baby?

If you were one of Joan Jett and the Blackhearts would you be Joan or a Blackheart? (Remember 'I Love Rock 'n' Roll'? I sure do!)

What to do if you are a Retro Hetero:

☆ Men: Come on the Watford Warrior Weekend. You will learn about moisturising and kick-boxing.

> *See also* NEW VIRILITY.

☆ Women: Sign up for the Empowerment Workshop for Ladies. You will learn salsa and all about the Games That Men Play.

> *See also* LIPSTICK LEADERSHIP.

Roger Risk

SUCCEEDERS, welcome to an old and good friend, Roger Risk. Without Mr Risk there is no life and no BUZZNESS. What would you rather have in your life – risk or rusk? Babies eat rusk. Grown-ups eat risk. Which are you?

To Make Business Brisk, Take a Risk!

I took a risk by investing in a van and kitting it out for refrigerated transport. But pretty soon chilled distribution was all the rage. Then I took a risk by selling out and travelling. But enrolling at the Gualala Dolphin seminary in Northern California and fully immersing myself in Dolphin Mythology &

Esthetics [*Ned*: please note this is how Americans spell it, so it must be right] was one of the best things I ever did. I took a risk in getting married, which proves the point that not all risks are worth it. We'll see how Frankie B copes …

Role-Play

Where executives pretend to be a tree or someone in their team so as to find out what on earth they are doing. Or actors try to make sense of the emotional violence in an organisation by performing a sketch carefully written by a professional writer and then brilliantly rewritten by several middle-ranking functionaries in a lengthy phone conference. A mirror is held up to an organisation to see how it works.

Here are some of the titles that will be available from Succeed-e-Vision next year:

Leadership: Is It OK to Shout?
Conflict: It Needn't End up in Fisticuffs in the Car Park
Strategy: What on Earth Shall We Do Next?

Room Worker

Someone who can work the room like Elton John can play the piano, especially in 'Song for Guy'. He or she can get more BUZZNESS CARDS than I've had hot dinners – and thanks to my room-working abilities I've had quite a few.

Top Tips for Succeeder Room Working (SRW)

☆ Avoid low-net-worth individuals.
☆ Waiting staff are fair game (they could be the son or daughter of a rich or high-net-worth individual. If not, at least they can make sure you get plenty of finger food).

☆ The key is not just entering an interface, it's leaving as well.

How to End an Interface Once It Has Gone Beyond Its Usefulness

☆ I need to go to the toilet.
☆ Sorry, I've just seen someone I owe a phone call.
☆ It's been really inspiring meeting you.
☆ Hey, my drink needs freshening up – can I get you something?
☆ Sorry, I need to go and take my drugs now. I've only got two weeks to live, so I won't bother taking your business card.

Exercise

A highly NETWORTHY person (whom you have targeted for months) is talking to a member of the royal family. How do you butt in?

☆ Excuse me, Your Highness, this guy needs to talk to me.
☆ Hey, dude, it's your lucky day – you've met a prince and now you're meeting me.
☆ Look over there. One of your corgis is bothering David Essex.

Remember the FRIENDSHIP AUDIT? Well, you should be doing something similar at a preliminary level when Room Working. Here is a model for the sort of calculations you should be making. There are four types of interface:

1. **Taking** – I can get something from this person.

2. **Gotta Get outta Here** – This person can give me nothing.
3. **Could Go Either Way** – Maybe I can get something from this person.
4. **Win/Win/Win** – We could be good for each other.

Sales

Vital in today's FMBE. Without it you will die, literally. All the time you are selling something – mostly yourself. As a baby you have to sell yourself to your parents or they will give you away. Your father needs to be persuaded that you aren't the offspring of the milkman. At school we learn to sell to peers, to avoid Playground Anxiety. Then we have to sell ourselves to the opposite sex. Then it's time to sell ourselves into a job and then to customers and colleagues.

Selling Isn't Evil!

Research by Professor William Trankin of the Jimmy Connors Institute of Business in San Diego found that without sales eventually things stop getting made.

SAS

Succeeder Action Squad. A crack unit of Succeederisers who can jet in to any organisation and administer a MOTIVITALITY CHECK. Though with Nikki absent we are a bit short at the moment.

Self-Coaching

A SUCCEEDER is great at Self-Coaching. Nowadays, there is plenty of training accessible through the medium of video. No longer is it a question of gathering everyone in the canteen and projecting a film onto the wall. We can all download video to our phones or laptops. Self-Coaching can be done anywhere. L-Vo has done a series of training videos too – Succeed-e-Vision. You may have a BlackBerry or an iPhone on which you could watch them. We are working on a proto-type, called the L-Vone, a mobile device for the Succeeder, with Succeeder ringtones and prompts (*see* SUCCEEDER SOUNDS) to enhance the possibilities for Self-Coaching. You'll be able to download Succeeder ringtones (*see* Appendices) and it will tell you when another Succeeder is nearby so you can exchange BUZZNESS CARDS and do some impromptu Self-Coaching with each other.

Shaving

Vital in today's fast-moving business environment (FMBE), especially for men. Are you ready to join the Shavy Train to Success? How long do you spend shaving? Men might spend twenty-seven minutes a day; that's about a week per year. Shaving is an investment in your future, so seek the best ROI (Return on Investment; but you could think of it as ROS – Return on Shav-estment). To help you, we're talking to Bill Turnbull of BBC *Breakfast* about hosting a Succeeder Skin-care Seminar at Watford Colosseum next year, with an excit-ing breakout demonstrating the new Succeeder Stubble razor – one that isn't very efficient, so leaving you with the rugged-but-not-a-beard look.

See APPENDICES *for more products for men and women.*

Sistas of Success

See LIPSTICK LEADERSHIP. Find out more about Sista Succeeder
She-Shave in the Appendices.

Six Sigma

A very clever methodology in BUSINESS created by somebody
in America that provides the answer to all sorts of problems.
I have gone beyond the traditional approach. I use Five
Sigma – it saves time. It's nearly 17 per cent more efficient.

Slogan

If you were a product, what would your slogan be? Think of
some great ones, like:

> Coke Adds Life!
> Don't Be Needy, Be Succeedy!
> We're up Hanley, Duck! (Signal Radio, Stoke-on-Trent)

You need to think of your strengths and what differentiates
you from others. For example:

> Hi, I'm Vic. I can do it!
> I'm Jeremy. I can handle supply chains and I'm nice.
> Hello, I'm Teresa. You won't find anybody better than
>   me at management accounting in this postcode.

Does Your Slogan
Wake You up Like Wogan?

Spellology

The profound understanding that words may contain more
than their meaning. It's like numerology, the study of the
mysterious and hidden meaning of numbers, but for letters

instead. (We're also working on a letter version of Sudoku called SUCCEEDOKU). Letters are important, without a doubt. There's plenty of talk these days about the Learning Organisation, but perhaps the priority should be about being an Earning Organisation. A difference of but one letter, yet an organisation that's not *earning* is one that may not be able to do much *learning* pretty soon … Other than about how to dole out the P45s.

And look at the word SUCCEEDER: three Es; two Cs; but only one U! … Only one <u>You</u>!

SQ

SUCCEEDER Quotient. A bit like IQ or EQ only more Succeedy. What's yours? Take the preliminary test. Score your answers to the questions below like this:

Strongly agree: (1)

Neither agree nor disagree: (2)

Strongly disagree: (3)

I've got goals.

I know who I am.

I'm on top of my hair.

I'm a role model to myself.

I can see far.

I eat right.

People want to hang with me.

I am fully hydrated.

I am comfortable with my manliness/womanliness.

I haven't been on a Succeeder Weekend but I would really like to.

How did you score?

Less than 11	Well done. You have high SQ. But could you have done better? Why not try a *Succeeder* Weekend?
Less than 18	Hmm. Moderate SQ. Don't you want to lower your score? Come on a Succeeder Weekend.
More than 18	Crikey. You really need to come on a Succeeder Weekend.
23 or more	Call me now! I can arrange a Succeeder Emergency Pit-Stop immediately.

Status Quo

Many of us in the Success Community are always looking to attack the status quo. Fair enough, but don't attack Status Quo, the world's greatest rockers! Their songs can be of enormous help to us in the PDB World. The lyrics have profound meaning. Were the Quo not at the forefront of globalisation with 'Rockin' All over the World'? They didn't just like it – they li-ii-ii-iked it! Often in negotiations I remember the thoughtful words of 'What You're Proposin'' ('Just once or twice, and not disclosin''). If anyone from Marketing is having problems understanding that the consumer decides all, I refer them to 'Whatever You Want' ('You pay your money, you take your choice'). Where teamwork is an issue, I ask people to focus on the fact that they are all fighting together ('You're in the Army Now'). These lessons are well worth learning 'Again again again again again again again again.' Remember that next time you want to 'Get Down Deeper and Down'!

Step-Change

A big change. This is a dancing metaphor – it requires a lot to change your step. And LEADERSHIP is like a dance: you need to listen, keep moving and beware of treading on people's toes. That's why I encourage leaders to go on my Dance to the Main Chance Workshops. Using the metaphor of dance and EXPERIENTIAL LEARNING experiences, with coaching from professional dancers who auditioned for *Strictly Come Dancing*, we unlock movement metaphors with modules such as:

> When to Lift – When to Spin
> Do You and Your Team Share the Same Rhythm?
>   (remember, Guilty Feet Have Got No Rhythm)
> Cha-Cha-Cha – The Right Way to Handle Compliance
>   Issues?

NB A sea-change is much bigger than a step-change, just like a sea is bigger than a step, but both are essential in BUZZNESS.

Strategy

The thing you are going to do. That's what you tell stakeholders anyhow. I find many leaders who are strategically restless. So we have a Session on Succeeder Strategising (SOSS). It begins with a game of Off-Ground Tick, to loosen limbs and to activate everyone's NEURO BUREAU. We warm up with some Blue-Sky Thinking, then graduate to some Out-of-the-Box Musing and finally get down to some No-Holds-Barred Brainstorming (or Thoughtshowering, as I prefer to call it). It's a thrilling roller-coaster ride of CREATIVISING and everyone comes out with a new strategy. It's been so successful that many clients haven't asked me to come back.

'My company was in paper distribution. As a result of the SOSS, I realised we should be making sports day trophies.'

Mike, Wheathampstead

'I sensed our timelines were all wrong. Now I am looking at thirty-five-year plans and not worrying about next week.'

Fay, Hemel Hempstead

'Thanks to the session, I sacked everybody in my team. Then I got sacked myself. It's the best thing that ever happened to me. I think.'

Jacob, Biggleswade

Stress

Is your workforce stressed and fearful? I sense you are as well, probably. Time to do something about it. I divide my week up in the following way: CHILL DAYS and Stress Days. But not just any stress – Successful Stress or SUCC-STRESS.

A Chill Day is when you have no meetings or deadlines. Make sure you have at least two per week. Load all the stress on to the other days. I love stress but I also love chill, yet never the twain shall meet. On a Chill Day, I rise late, wear loose saffron-coloured clothes, have carrot juice for breakfast and visualise kayaking to work. On a Succ-Stress Day, I rise early, dress in black and load up with good carbs. Remember this:

Without Stress, You're Gonna Get in a Mess
Without Chill, You're Gonna Get Ill!

Succ-Stress Days can be further divided into DONKEY DAYS and WOW DAYS. Wow Days are for BUZZNESS breakthroughs. Donkey Days are for dull donkey work. Here are suggestions.

Chill Day Top up the NEURO BUREAU. phone friends. Drink vegetable juice. Chant. Watch *Neighbours* (twice – at 1.45 p.m., then again at 5.30 p.m.). Play tennis.

Donkey Day Pay bills, pick up dry-cleaning, try to get internet connection working.

Wow Day Pitches, presentations, strategising. Have major HOCUS-FOCUS.

Structure (of Presentations)

Say what you're going to say, say that you've said it, then say it again but differently.

SucceeDance

We know about the musical *Riverdance*, which so eloquently tells the story of the ascent of man through tap-dancing and Irish jigging. Well, I'm writing a musical called *SucceeDance*, which is a fable of the ascent of one man from suburban no-hoper to global guru (via refrigerated transport and a heck of a lot of soul-searching). We are considering who will play the lead. Michael Flatley and George Clooney are both in the frame. We're just waiting for their agents to call us back. Already plans are under way for a production at the Queen Mother Theatre, Hitchin.

Succeeder

One who succeeds. And Success is how YOU choose to define it, not me.

Do You Know Your Definition of Success?

You may feel it is simply getting through the day, rather than power, money or fame. But one day you will realise what proper Success is. See VENN DIAGRAM OF MOTIVITALITY.

'There are no traffic cops on the freeway to Succeedership. Only the ones you create.'

L. Vaughan Spencer

Case Study

Jenni was under stress and under-confident. She went on a Succeeder© Course. Now she is married and is the chief executive of a big company.

Succeeder Fingers

See the front cover of this book. This may be hard while reading, so it is probably best to go and buy another copy and continue reading later. You might like to think about buying another two, so that you have one at home, one at the office and one in your car.

You make an L-shape with your first finger and thumb. Remember, L is for Love, Life and L-Vo. Use the Succeeder Fingers in the SUCCEEDER GREETING and for achieving HOCUS-FOCUS. Here are some other occasions to use it:

☆ Before a first date.
☆ Before giving a presentation.
☆ When meeting the Queen.
☆ When collecting an award for services to humanity or for conspicuous coaching bravery in the face of intractable issues.

Succeeder Greeting

The secret signal between people who have been to a SUC-CEEDER Workshop. This involves the SUCCEEDER FINGERS pointing at the eyes, with strong eye contact. Don't be put off if people don't know how to take it. You'll soon meet someone who does, after a couple of months or years.

Succeeder Institute

A think tank where we do much of our best thinking. It is funded by the Hertfordshire Creative Campaign for Commercial Excellence and by private donations – mentioning no names! We give awards and bursaries. For example, we sponsored the Skybrook Primary School Under-Fives' Business Innovation Scheme, where creative youngsters come up with top BUZZNESS ideas. One enterprising boy had the idea of running a spread-betting index on whose mum would arrive latest at the school gates in the afternoon. He was awarded a certificate and his dad was given a bottle of sparkling wine. We also sponsor an intern at the Luton Nail Salon.

Succeeder No

A Negative No can sound horrid and put people off. A Succeeder No is light and friendly and impresses people because of its assertiveness.

Practise your Succeeder No:

1. Smile.
2. Open your heart.
3. Be positive.
4. Open your arms.
5. Put your thumbs up.

6. Think of a positive cheery role model (e.g. Declan Curry ex-BBC *Breakfast*).

Remember, a Succeeder No (with open-heart chakra) is better than a bad yes or a Negative No (with no chakra at all). Practise it now – with your colleagues, family or traffic wardens.

Succeederology

The Science of Success. Yes, SUCCESS is a science. It's tried and tested – not in a test tube, but in the white heat of experience. Easy as 1 + 1. And here is the formula – the Two-Step Process (TSP)

1. Have a Goal.
2. Achieve It.

This is a bit like the Eight-Step Programme but it's quicker. People will try and complicate things, but it's as simple as that. So you don't have to be the best that you might be. You don't have to be the best that someone else is. Forget best. Just be better than you are.

Succeeder Silence

See QUIET TIME

Succeeder Solstice

Traditionally people observe the summer solstice. The SUC-CEEDER celebrates the Succeeder Solstice (6 November) on the anniversary of the day when I first invented the ancient science of SUCCEEDEROLOGY (and unlike the other solstices, it doesn't clash with school holidays or GCSEs). Why not come to our next ceremony? Please bring a cushion and a

Succeeder Sacrifice (packed lunch). A small collection will be taken to cover expenses (for the fire-eater and marshmallows).

'After the Succeeder Solstice Ceremony, everything fell into place – I got a new job, a new relationship and, most importantly, a new hairstyle. Now I know there is magic in my voice.'

Natasha, ex-trapeze artiste

'It finished too quickly! I could have gone on for another three days! I feel liberated. Certainly everyone at work has noticed the difference.'

Mike, traffic warden

'After the group chant sessions, which we now use every morning, we found our profits went up 6.7 per cent, thanks mostly to letting go members of staff whose chanting was deemed substandard.'

Chris, CEO Watford Crystals and Inner Healing Bookshop

Succeeder Sound(s)

Every day we are surrounded by sounds, many of them outside our control. But what if we were to rewrite the script? From first thing in the morning, when your alarm goes off, and then throughout the day, when your phone rings, you can be subject to a nobler noise. Here are some examples available from the L. Vaughan Spencer Foundation:

Alarm/Wake-up Call: Motivitalising Morning Messages recorded by L-Vo

'Wake up to Success.'

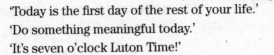

'Today is the first day of the rest of your life.'

'Do something meaningful today.'

'It's seven o'clock Luton Time!'

Succeeder Moti-Mixed Ringtones

'Succeeder!' (to tune of 'Tequila').

'Succeedy Like Sunday Morning' (to the tune of the Commodores' 'Easy Like Sunday Morning', covered so brilliantly by Faith No More).

'I Should Be Succeedy' (to the tune of 'I Should Be So Lucky').

For more, *see* Appendices.

Succeeder Doorbell Messages

'Ding-dong – Time to network.'

'Knock-knock – Here comes opportunity.'

'Let me into your house. Let me into your life!'

We are working on messages for the ringee, like:

'Coming ready or not!'

'The door to Success is about to open!'

Succeeder Triangle

The area bounded by the triad of Watford, Luton and Stevenage. We can match anything in Silicon Valley. They've got Hewlett-Packard, Apple and eBay. We've got London Luton Airport!

See map on page viii.

Succeediness©

The state of mind and body that surpasses traditional Success, through the medium of Personal Self-Enhancement. This can only be achieved by attending SUCCEEDER Workshops and buying Succeeder CDs, videos and clothing (*see* Appendices for more details; *see also* VENN DIAGRAM OF MOTIVITALITY).

Succee-Do

The Martial Art of Motivitality. Aikido is the Way of Harmony. Kendo is the Way of the Sword. Succee-Do is the Way of Success. I asked my colleague Mandy, who is an ex-dancer, so knows about movement and the body, to create a specific discipline for the SUCCEEDER. Kendo (named after Kendo Nagasaki, the wrestler) became Can-Do became Succee-Do. It's easier than Kendo, because it doesn't involve bamboo swords and protective clothing. We use imaginary swords and Succeeder T-shirts.

Succeedoku

Almost like Sudoku but based on letters.

S	U	C		E		D	E	R	S
C									
									C
E									
E									
									D
S			C					R	S

Can you fill in the missing letters?

Success & Succeediness

This is the journal I started which is dedicated to research into the Science of SUCCEEDEROLOGY. This month, for example, our most downloaded articles are:

'Testosterone: Necessary but Not Sufficient?'

Interview with the Nigel Venture, CEO of Stevenage
    Enterprise Body and Keen Freemason

'Why I Wish I Were a Woman', Chris Akabusi (*not the*
    athlete). He's spelt Kriss.

'Skybrook: How a Primary School Can Become a Profit
    Centre Using Spread-Betting'

So far the readership is confined to select members of the local Success Community. I've asked for contributions but reaction has been a bit thin on the ground. Mandy's working on something about 'Breathing and Business' and I wrote to the boss of the CBI for his thoughts on the exciting outlook for the SUCCEEDER TRIANGLE but nothing's come back yet. He doesn't seem to have been tempted by the fact that we pay £5 for 2,000 words (plus SUCCEEDER T-shirt). I'm hoping to get it distributed by WH Smith next year. They have everything the BUZZNESS person needs – magazines, Post-it notes and felt tips. Our most popular article ever remains the interview with Nick Owen and his Top Ten tips on 'Dressing for Business Success'.

Success-o-Phobe(s)

One who is utterly terrified of Success. He or she suffers from Succeedy Deficit Disorder (SDD) and is a Saboteur of Success, for it scares him or her more than FAILURE. Failure, while being a useful pontoon across the RIVER OF RAGE, a base camp on the Ascent to Achievement, is no place to tarry. Thank goodness I am not there.

Quiz: Are You a Success-o-Phobe?

1. A colleague says, 'Well done!' to you for a project. Do you:
   - (a) Say thanks
   - (b) Spend a quarter of an hour telling them why it wasn't really that good
2. Your boss offers you a pay rise. Do you:
   - (a) Accept graciously
   - (b) Point out who else deserves it instead
3. You are selected to be featured in the company's in-house magazine. Do you:
   - (a) Choose a new outfit for the photo
   - (b) Resign immediately.

Succ-Stress

SUCCEEDER Stress. Vital in today's fast-moving modern business environment (FMMBE). Use it, embrace it, channel it. Then have a CHILL DAY.

See also STRESS.

Synergy

Something that everything and everyone must have – people, products, parking lots. Two or more elements working well

Mostly (a): Don't worry – you are normal.
Mostly (b): You have a bad case of SDD – come and visit the Succeeder Surgery!

together (rather than in opposition) to create WIN/WIN/WIN. I love the Energy of Synergy. Here are some examples:

Salt & Pepper
Salt 'n' Pepa
Chaka Demus & Pliers
Surf 'n' Turf
Sir Alan Hansen & Sir Alan Shearer
Emerson, Lake & Palmer (they Win/Win/Win/Win!)
Hoddle & Waddle
Fern (Britton) & Philip (Schofield)
Chas 'n' Dave

Here are just some examples of Succeeder Synergy I have created for my clients:

☆ Hungry customers of Luton Futon get a free cake (from Nice Buns) with every purchase.

☆ Luton Fridge Shelf Replacements offer a low-cost warranty underwritten by Luton & Beds Insurance.

☆ Exhaust-o-Cure offer discounted exhausts to anyone displaying a 'Find Your Fun in Stevenage' sticker on their car.

Synergy Is Win-ergy!

Talent Management

Making sure your good-looking employees don't leave – or all end up in the same department! No, but seriously, it's hard to hold on to your best people. I should know – I've lost Nikki, it would appear. And got Liam, part-time, though he does seem to be doing rather well in selling SUCCEEDER T-shirts.

See also WAR ON TALENT.

Team/(Team-building)

According to research by Professor Trankin of the Jimmy Connors Institute of Business, a team is more than one person but less than infinity.

Is yours a Dream Team or a Slack Pack? Is your crew at their peak or terminally weak? Are they Under-MotivitaliseD (UMD)? Are they like ants without any pants? King Arthur and his Knights without a round table? Or a flock of seagulls but not in a flock? Where can we look for examples of best practice in teamwork? How about professional soccer – the Premier League? Players are overpaid, have no loyalty to the organisation and don't work for two months of every year.

See any parallels with your outfit? Remember, PDB professional, be strong! Fight fire with facilitation!

Case Study

A team wasn't working well. Then they came for a Succeeder
Squad Session (SSS). Now they are working well and making
Motivational Muffins for each other every Friday.

A non-performing team is like a family sitting in a car not
moving. Pretty soon, the windows steam up. They can't see
what's going on outside. What to do? They can either stop
breathing or wind down the window.

For most organisations, the first is not an option (though
some seem to manage in the hospitality industry!) So it's time
to let in some fresh air. That's what I am: a breath of hot air. I
am like having your own wind. I am your Wind of Change and
I smell good. I can evaporate the condensation of low motivation so you can you see the bigger picture outside. So, is your
posse teaming up or 'steaming up'? This table will tell you.

TEAMING UP	STEAMING UP
Holding hands	Holding grudges
Hugging	Bugging
Baking	Belly-aching
Having drinks	Making threatening comments and sending vicious emails

Traditional team theories are one croissant short of a
business breakfast. To create a team you have to be united in
one thing – it can be hate or love. Professor Krench and I
have summarised the way in which all teams achieve cohe-
sion (see below). There are no exceptions.

The Four-by-Four Team Table

	Everyone	Someone
Likes	ELE: Everyone likes everyone	ELS: Everyone likes someone
Hates	EHE: Everyone hates everyone	EHS: Everyone hates everyone

Which one is your team? Are you the Someone?

Television

At the moment I am talking to backers about launching SUC-CEEDER TV (twenty-four-hour motivitalising TV beamed or streamed direct into your digital receiver). I'd use real proper motivators, not the prissy, poster boys YBM. There's a small warehouse next door at the Spring Lakes Business Park, which could easily be a studio, and one of the parents at Skybrook is a freelance assistant cameraman. Apparently he did that advert that's constantly on daytime TV where they encourage you to sue people who've made you fall over bits of pavement or dropped things on your head at work. And Mandy knows several actresses from her time being an extra on *Midsomer Murders*. I was on *Watchdog* once when somebody wanted their money back from a SUCCEEDER Weekend but they hadn't read the small print, which quite clearly states that we only *hope* that you will be running your own business and in a relationship a month after the course. In Canada, I had my own TV chat show, called *Let Go with L-Vo*, which won an award for Best Middle-of-the-Night Cable Talk Show in a Non-Metropolitan Area.

Nowadays I don't watch much TV (apart from *Neighbours*, for research purposes). I'll try to catch the things that are relevant to my work, like *Working Lunch*, *The Money*

Programme and *Trinny & Susannah*. I've just found this show from America called *Extreme Biz*. It's presented by Garrett (a former boxer, now the owner of a global childrens wear empire) and Chuck (who was brought up by wolves, then did his MBA at the Shark School of Business in Florida). They have a day to turn around a business by installing innovative business techniques or sacking staff. Invariably there are tears of joy or pain or both. It's riveting.

Nowadays, business is often on television in shows like *Dragons' Den*, but the wily trainer knows that there is plenty to learn about BUZZNESS from other TV shows. For example:

Match of the Day

It's important to celebrate success. Jumping on top of each other, kissing each other, taking off your shirt and then running around twirling it. Why can't this be done in any office, call centre or operating theatre?

Britain's Got Talent

Finding the right people means trawling through rubbish.

Deal or No Deal

It's important to remember that business involves a lot of guess-work.

Who Wants to Be a Millionaire?

It's OK to phone a friend for advice sometimes. Or ask a group of nearby strangers.

Weakest Link

Never trust someone who's had too much plastic surgery.

Tennis

A great metaphor for business (and life) … You start with love, then service, there are backhanders, sometimes you just can't stand the racket and your faults are pointed out loudly by others, sometimes you're in, sometimes you're out. And don't forget to have a banana when you change ends. To learn more, why not come on our 'Tennis for Succeeders Intensive'? Not only do you learn to play the big points and keep your nerve in the tie-break, but, thanks to our fitness regime with Coach Mandy, you will look great in tennis shorts.

You'll also learn that life is the best of five sets. And that things are easier with a partner. Not that I have one right now. I feel like I double-faulted through a whole game. Unfortunately, the manageress of the Luton Nail Salon misunderstood my reference to doubles last week. Maybe I crossed the baseline. I went to the net, but the loneliness continues.

Testimonial

When you've done a good job, ask your customer for a testimonial. It will impress potential clients and reminds the original client how good you were. That's if they thought you were good. Don't pass on negative feedback. I don't tend to get any and, if I do, it's normally because of factors beyond my control. For example, why didn't they tell me most of the audience were German at that car plant in Frankfurt? My hilarious jokes about beach towels normally go down a storm.

Here are some examples of test manuals I've had:

'L. Vaughan Spencer was such a good host and keynote speaker at our national conference that I immediately

booked him to speak at all forty-three of our exhaust-fitting centres across Wales and the South-West. Not an easy task, but through a combination of shouting and outdoor motivational exercises involving spanners, he succeeded in raising levels of SUCCEEDINESS *even among the most cynical participants. Some were so quickly transformed that they went home early.'*

Simon, Regional Manager, Exhaust-o-Cure

'I found L-Vo nourishing on many levels.'

Sandra, Letchworth

'When I first met L-Vo I was a hard-working over-achiever. I used to worry so much about money. Now L-Vo has relieved me of much of that.'

Charles, former CEO of Brainbox Software, now known
as Soaring Squirrel

'He is the Banksy of Business. If business is the new rock 'n' roll, he is Led Zep of Leadership – the Meta-Physical Graffiti on the Stadium Walls of Commerce. The Supply Chain Doesn't Remain the Same. He's got a Whole Lotta Love. He's the Stairway to Hi-Octane Hi-Achievin' Heaven.'

Chuck Tippetts, Global Achiever, CEO Global Achievements Inc.,
Tallahassee, Florida

'I certainly was keen to use my cleaver by the end of a day with him.'

Mike Coulson, Head Chopper, Dunstable Abattoir

'He can transform failing organisations just by looking at the car park. He loves the Fizzness of Business (as he

calls it). He's never satisfied with mediocrity. He's fearless. Forget the jargon, the mystery, the flim-flam. He tells it how he is.'

Rita Kewl, Nice Buns Bakery, Hitchin

'Where did you find this bloke?'

Sergeant Hardrada, Bucks and Beds Police

Thinking

To be done outside a BOX. How did I revolutionise the chilled distribution industry? By Thinking Outside the Ice-Box (see article in *Success & Succeediness*: 'The Cool Chain is one that is both complex and simple. To transport food to where it has to be *and* keep it cold requires a surgeon's eye for precision, an artist's feel for nature and dancer's feel for logistics').

But what is your box? Isn't it better sometimes to stop thinking and look at the box more carefully? Is there a jack in it? Or does it belong to Pandora? And what may look like a box to you could look like a treasure chest to someone else (especially if they are a pirate).

Find Out More About the Box Before Thinking Outside It!

Ticking

To be done to boxes, though not ones outside which people are thinking, says Frederick.

TLA

Three-Letter Acronym. Vital in today's fast-moving modern business environment (FMMBE). Four-or-More-Letter Acronyms (FOMLA) can make an even bigger difference. There are plenty of examples of TLAs and FOMLAs in the Appendices.

Toilet Break

Vital in today's fast-moving modern training environment (FMMTE) – and often when the best interfaces occur. But people are very slow coming back from them, especially smokers now they have to go outside. Remember – 3 per cent of business is done in the toilet. No, not that sort of business. Sadly, I have found senior executives hiding in the toilet drinking miniatures from their mini-bar or playing football with one of my handouts rolled up into a ball during some of our more challenging interventions, like URBAN TRIBAL DRUMMING or Finding Deep MEANINGFULNESS in Project Management. And there's T-Learning, of course, where this 'downtime' can be used more effectively.

See also LEARNING.

Tong Shui ©

See FENG SHUI *and* HAIR. The role that hair plays in Success. Often overlooked by traditional business writers.

Training

To be a trainer means being in the front line. You're under attack – from the cannons of corporate cost-cutting and the blunderbusses of boardroom brigadiers. Management manoeuvres may leave your flank exposed. Truly L&D means Live & Die. Those who live by the blackboard may die by the sword. It's kill or be killed. You're a fighter pilot, in a dogfight to the death over the Fields of Failure.

Are You Winning the Battle?
Don't Surrender Your Agenda

So next time you're summoned to a meeting with senior management, remember to pack some heat (that means taking a gun in street-talk. I don't mean this literally, except in the most extreme of cases, like in the world of stationery supply). Be armed with up-to-the-minute stats. You're the cavalry, arriving with the outcomes of a skills workshop to terrify the enemy. Mention a little performance management here, a sales module there, a nugget of negotiation way over there and you're fully aligned, your foes vanquished in a volley of Lean Five Sigma. When the going gets tough, the trainers get training. I love the smell of flip-chart in the morning!

Many people ask me, 'What's the difference between training and coaching?' The answer is in the words. Think of the difference between a train and a coach. A train involves more people, it goes on straight lines and you can walk around. With a coach, there may not be a toilet. That just about sums up the differences. Training may involve a trolley service of drinks and light refreshments.

If You Don't Train
Your Brain's in the Drain!

Training (of Trainers)

Vital in any organisation in today's fast-moving modern business environment (FMMBE). Without training there is no life. But who trains the trainers (T2)? And who trains the people who train the trainers who train the trainers (T4)? And who trains them (T5 – but don't think Heathrow!)? It's exhausting even thinking about it, isn't it? So if you want the best training for your trainers, come to the SUCCEEDER INSTITUTE. Our training, 'Train the Trainers Who Train the Trainer-Trainers', is second to none.

'The "Train the Trainers Who Train the Trainer-Trainers" course was very fun and left me full of Motivitality though a bit tired.'

Zoe Sproule, Abercromby District Council (Chief Succeedy Officer)

Transformation

Something we are all aiming at. With Professor Krench of Succeeder Lab, I have identified the Process of Transformation. Here it is:

1. Wanting to transform.
2. Identifying how to transform.
3. Transforming.
4. Checking that you have transformed.

Most people make the mistake of missing out a step. Or not knowing which step they are on. Or forgetting number 4. How do you know that you have transformed? Certainly, people are constantly surprised by how I look. That's personal transformation. What about corporate transformation? Here are some of our latest exciting ones:

Recent Succeeder Solutions Interventions

Client	What we did to them
Hitchin Crematorium	Made them buck up their ideas and pull up their socks
Harpenden Bowls Club	Reimagined their car park
St Albans Hauliers	Taught them all URBAN TRIBAL DRUMMING – and thus fearlessness
Spiritual Alchemy Associates	Helped them deal with the trauma of having a new carpet
North Mimms Tree Fellers	Enhanced LEADERSHIP Bandwidth

Trendologist

Someone who can see the future of commerce. At the SUC-CEEDER INSTITUTE we do a lot of research into Trendology, predicting the major trends – the Turbo-Trends – that will set the agenda in the 22ND CENTURY. They used to make cars in Luton. Now they make industrial fasteners. Maybe your dad was a car mechanic. Your daughter will be a quantum mechanic and your granddaughter a karma mechanic!

Pretty soon the trad job won't exist. Typist – bye! Factory worker – ciao! Book-keeper – auf Wiedersehen! Jobs are evolving as we speak. Apparently, Liam wants to study the Semiotics of Social Networks. He's on Bebo and uses it to sell his SUCCEEDER ringtones, which seem to be doing rather well.

We have entered the Digital Age. Pretty soon, we'll be entering the Age of Enlighten-up-ment, where emotion and spirituality will be more important than ironmongery and hardware. Are you ready to upgrade your Succeeder software?

Forget Civil Engineer – Think Empathy Engineer!

Forget Blacksmith – Think Succeedersmith!

Imagine the scene in 2018, when everyone has read this book. This will be a typical day for the average BUZZNESS person.

06.00 Rise
07.00 Self-Appreciation
08.00 Jog to work or car-share (car run on solar or wind power or cocoa butter)
09.00 WARM-UP
09.15 Conversations with Colleagues
09.30 Conversations with Customers
09.45 Conversations with Stake-Holders
10.30 Conversation with Self
11.00 Tea-break (or 'Hunger Break' for world poverty, if this hasn't been solved)
11.15 CREATIVISING
11.30 YO-YOGA
11.45 Invoicing
12.00 Blue-Sky Thinking
13.00 Lunch
13.45 Watercooler Empathy Moment
14.00 Forgiveness
14.15 Training Newbies
15.00 Self-Appraisal
15.15 Light Reading
15.45 Phone a Friend You Haven't Spoken to for Ages
16.00 Visualisation
16.15 Tea-break (drink eight glasses of desalinated, revitaminised water)

16.30 Goal-Focusing for Tomorrow
16.50 Collecting your receipts into an envelope
17.00 Go home
17.30 Watch *Neighbours* projected on a plasma
cupboard

22nd Century

Where business is headed – without a doubt. Make sure you get there first.

24/7

How business is conducted today … it's round the clock, it's global. My own business is spreading. I now have a client in Harrow. India is hours ahead of us, as are China and Russia, but Brazil is behind us. That's why I'm in Luton, a useful halfway house.

And 24/7 is my commitment to you, if you decide to become one of my Premium Coaching Clients. You can call me any time of the day or night. Try to call during the day, though, if possible. If I've turned my phone off I'll call back in the morning. And you get a free SUCCEEDER pen. (Introductory Offer: £1,700 if you use the code 'Yes, I'm Ready.')

'I attended the Premium Coaching Event.'

Darren Walsall, Chief Executive, Fight Stores (Luton High Street branch)

Über-Guru

Yes, I know the *Financial Times* called me this (26 September 2006), perhaps because of my exalted position in the PDB universe and because I am blazing a trail, but I am just a guy doing his job. Call me an Über-Guru if you really really must, but I just found myself in the right place at the right time saying the right things for a competitive fee. Sure, people say I am a cross between Rudy Giuliani, the Dalai Lama and Jay-Zee, but I'm just doing my best, and if people want to list me in their top 100 trainers in the SUCCEEDER TRI-ANGLE or nominate me for awards or honours like an OBE for my services to business and personal development and education, I really can't stop them.

Uncle Uncertainty

He's always hanging around any organisation, whether it be large or small, in the profit or not-for-profit sector. Uncle Uncertainty is an old friend – or enemy, as you see it. Reframe him as your chum, along with AUNTIE AMBIGUITY and Colin Complexity, wrong-footing your rivals, but giving you a competitive advantage, a gap to be exploited through Ian

Innovation. Be nimble and Bob's your uncle (as well as Uncle Uncertainty).

Understand the Upside of Uncertainty!

Upside

See DOWNSIDE.

Upskill

Making someone better at their job, through Learning and Development. You take them to the next level. Here's a table that shows what Learning and Development can really do.

Current Level	Next Level
Can write proposal	Can run a project
Can hold her own at parties	Major-league ROOM WORKER
SUCCEEDER	Master Succeeder
Chief Executive	Executive Coach
Face Washer	Expert in pre-shave skin scrub, post-shave balm and evening moisturiser

Urban Tribal Drumming (UTD)

Drumming to motivitalise TEAM spirit and individual HOCUS-FOCUS. We run courses in UTD, to loosen the creative juices, or at industrial tribunals as an alternative to traditional conciliation. Here are some modules:

Chill-Beats for Change

Beats to Groove the Office Move

Acoustic Accountancy

'The Urban Tribal Drumming really brought us together and now everyone is nice to each other.'

Stephanie Croak, Harpenden Debt Collectors

USP

1. Unique Selling Proposition or Point

Vital in today's fast-moving modern business environment (FMMBE). What is the USP of Brand You? What is L-Vo's? Well, there is nobody like me because nobody else in the Success Community has my combo of hair, clothing and rapping rapport.

Write your USP here ....

I am unique because ....

You may find it hard to think of anything that makes you noteworthy in any way, so here are some suggestions: your name, your address, your medical history.

Sign your name here ....

How about your organisation's USP? Here are some examples from the companies I have worked with:

Nice Buns Bakery – There's nowhere else you can get bread for a mile

Fight Stores – We're helping to facilitate fighting across Bedfordshire

Luton Learn to Drive – We're helping people learn to drive in the Luton area

Find Your Fun in Stevenage – Nobody else is doing it

2. Über Succeedy Pants

How old is the underwear you're wearing right now? If it's more than six months old, says Professor Krench, throw it away. Success starts at your centre. If you are wearing your SUCCEEDER Pants anything is possible. Wear them even on DRESS-DOWN FRIDAY.

Utopian

Thinking way too far out of the BOX. But if that's the charge, then I declare myself guilty, your honour. Sometimes you gotta dream big to get big. I did it with chilled distribution and now I'm doing it with SUCCEEDEROLOGY. Charles did it by quitting his job and family. Utopia is shorthand for the ideal society. Where would you be in your ideal world? How is Brand You doing? Think You-Topia. Start doing it now!

> *Are You Ready for You-Topia?*
> *Or Have You Got Motivational Myopia?*

Venn Diagram of Motivitality

We in the Success Community get a hard time from the cynical British press, which likes to make out that we're just out to make a quick buck. No way! SUCCEEDINESS is about more than money. Here's why:

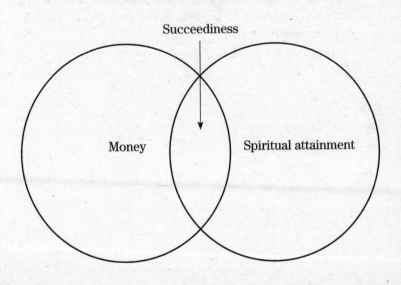

Succeediness

Money   Spiritual attainment

Voice – the V

We all have an inner voice, don't we? What's yours telling you? Is it unhelpful stuff, ELF-TALK, like:

> I'm going to be found out soon
> I don't deserve this success
> What's the French for croissant?

Time to rewrite the script. Let it be:

> I am Succeedy, I am Succeedy, Succeedy is Me

Let this be your internal Voice – 'the V' or SUCCEEDER Inner Voice (SIV). Try it now. Practise in front of the mirror at home, or when you are driving, or communally at the Monday morning team meeting. Much of my coaching work is to quash the ELF and reframe (through P-THINK) the Script of the V. Many of my most successful one-on-one sessions are held in total silence, sometimes for hours on end, with occasional exchanges of the sign of the V. If you do this too, things will never be the same again. I guarantee your firm's revenue will increase by at least 17 per cent in the next quarter (unless other factors interfere).

Look out for the sign of the V!

Walk the Talk

Maybe you're ready to talk the talk. But can you walk the talk? It's no good just buying this book and reading it. Buying another copy may help. And another. But once you've bought, say, four copies it's time to get up and do something about it. You are now near the end of this book. Has anything changed? If not, I think you need to go and buy another copy and read it again. That's what Charles did. Once he had bought seventy-three copies of the book and read them all twice, he knew he had to walk right out of his old life. It might take a lifetime to apply the lessons of this book. Certainly, it's taken me my whole life to get where I am today.

Warm-up

Vital before a presentation. But why just then? Sportspersons warm up before training and so should BUZZNESS people! At the L. Vaughan Spencer Foundation, we warm up every morning. Outdoors is best. It's good to be in touch with nature, so we do it in the car park. Sometimes it can be tricky if they're delivering pies to the pie distributor next door, but we make sure our bodies and breathing are truly ready for the day ahead. Nikki is excused, though, since she did her back in with Downward Dog (a yoga move). Perhaps I should have told her there was no need to woof. I also warm-down after work: fifteen minutes of intense stretching in the car park. I did get jeered by some schoolgirls once. So now I do it in the lobby. The security man doesn't mind. I give him free copies of *Success & Succeediness*.

War on Talent

Big corporations have to fight for the best graduates from across the world. It's less a war (though there was that punch-up at that business school after the recruiter from a management consultancy told all the others, 'My back-end's bigger than yours') and more a sophisticated game of chess … Instead of pawns, knights and rooks, you have guarantees, foreign placements and non-domiciled tax benefits to play with.

Here's what to do if one of your star performers is head-hunted:

Tell them they are highly valued and ask what might
    persuade them to stay

Cry

Increase their pay

Give them a new job title

Get them a nicer outfit or nicer office to work in

Organise a better car-parking spot

Give them a bigger chair… Near the window

Tell them the company they are thinking of going to is
    rubbish and that they will get spat on by passers-by

I've tried all of these with Nikki – except increasing her pay. Really, the thing I have learned, and so should you, is that if someone wants to leave it's probably too late and so it's best to focus on darkening their reputation with colleagues.

Retention Is All About Attention!

I should have listened to Nikki when she said she wanted some training or some time off. I should have been more visible. I call this MBS – Management by Smiling. Wander round the office smiling at your people, giving them eye contact. This way, they will know how much you appreciate them and they can approach you if something's on their mind. You can then listen to them and try to deal with their beef, unless it's a pay rise.

Warrior

We all know that BUSINESS is war. Your BlackBerry is a spear. Your database is a sword. Invoices are armour and your BUZZNESS CARD is an intercontinental ballistic missile. Women have always understood this. That's why they wear warpaint. Men are coming round, and once again becoming the warriors we used to be – we put on our warpaint, e.g. GUYLINER, MOISTURISER and any amount of HAIR 'product'. We're getting left behind, because the only arena in which we get a chance to be a warrior is at a barbecue, reasserting our primeval family role as we wrestle red meat from the fridge and then burn it. Men have to create their role anew in the prevailing culture of CHICK-ITALISM.

So to make up for this Warrior Deficit I run the Watford Warrior Weekend. How often do you examine your manhood? It's time to say no to rampant maternalism as we re-establish the primeval paternalist pathway. So the Watford Warrior

Weekend is a crash course in NEW VIRILITY, held at the Ramada Jarvis Hotel on the A41. Modules include Skincare, SUCCEE-DO and Getting a Girlfriend (Then Keeping Her). Optional sessions are also held on Shaving, Manly Management and Knowing What to Say About Cars While Also Decrying Their Environmental Impact. You will learn how to War Dance on the War Path to Success.

Get there if you're a man – or if you've got one send him along. My dad said he was too busy to come (apparently it was an 'All-Poirot' Weekend on the Slippers-and-Pipe TV Channel), so I organised an Uncle and Nephew Weekend instead. Uncle Derek was terrific with a bivouac!

Water

Vital in today's fast-moving modern global business and management environment (FMMGBME). I drink eight glasses a day, though this can have consequences. Some of my best BUZZNESS thinking occurs while I am in the toilet; I find my NEURO-BUREAU really engages. Water is a great metaphor for business. If it's not moving, it goes stagnant. If it's not clean, it can cause disease. And nowadays people buy bottles of it when it used to be free.

Weekend

A time for many people to relax. But not the SUCCEEDER.
See also WORK-END.

White Collar

The traditional way of talking about those in management; the opposite of blue collar. My motto is Right Colour Collar (*see* COLOUR THERAPY).

Collar	Interpretation
Yellow	Not washed properly
Black with white dots	Needs 'Head and Shoulders'
Dog collar (white)	Vicar
Dog collar (studded)	Broad-minded
No collar	In advertising or athletics

Whisperer (Business)

Like a Horse Whisperer, but for BUSINESS. This is how I like to think of myself – a gentle, calming presence in a business, saying the right thing, creating powerful one-on-ones, with nobody really knowing what I am doing. I like to hear things from the horse's mouth, without frightening the horses. Business and horses have lots in common – there are plenty of one-trick ponies, some fall at the first fence and there's no shortage of mucking out to do.

Win/Win/Win

Nowadays people talk about Win/Win. That doesn't go far enough. There are other people who can win as well:

I Win …. You Win …. We Win

That's Win/Win/Win!

And sometimes They Win as well. That's Win/Win/Win/ Win!

WOM-Bat

Someone passing on word-of-mouth (WOM). Have you told your friends how good this book is? I bet they've noticed the change in you since you started reading it – the spring in your step, the glint in your eye or the mustard in your hot dog.

Work-End

Saturday and Sunday. Time for a different kind of work. The SUCCEEDER may work on family issues, the garden or hobbies. This is when I hold my Succeeder Workshops or do the work on myself that I haven't had time to do during the week because I've been so busy with others. What does this work consist of? Reading, laundry and the *Neighbours* omnibus on Five.

Wow Day(s)

As distinct from CHILL DAYS and DONKEY DAYS, this is SUCC-STRESS Day for doing things that make you (and others) go Wow! It's about creating and breaking new barriers. For example, on my next Wow Day (next week) I'm doing a new business pitch for a Leadership Programme for a firm of loss adjusters. Can't wait!

[I'm thinking of calling it the Loss Leader! *Ned*: I thought you would like this.]

Xmas

This is a dangerous time of year, what with office parties, mistletoe and card-sending. What does your Christmas card say about you? Everything we do is a symbol and you could be sending totally the wrong message. Beware! A picture of a dove says 'peace'. This is not good BUSINESS. It means you're a pushover in negotiations so it's better to have a huge polar bear. These guys eat raw meat – the original low-carb lunch! You won't find radicchio or celeriac at the North Pole. It's dog-eat-dog up there – or bear-eat-anything-that-moves. That's the way to do BUZZNESS. Take no prisoners and scoop up the little fish with one flash of your paw.

Sending a picture of Santa Claus is also a no-no – he's hardly aspirational! He's bloated, he gives things away for free, he can't control his workforce (Rudolph is clearly a candidate for realignment) and he's stuck in a niche market (Christmas comes but once a year).

A fun way to spice things up is to have a modern take on an old theme. Why not use a picture of the Three Wise Men but with recognisable faces superimposed – say, the judges from *X-Factor* or *Strictly Come Dancing* – Simon Cowell,

Craig Revel Horwood and Sharon Osbourne? This would show you're hip and up-to-date like me.

How about having handmade Christmas cards? I suggest outsourcing the project. Persuade your kid's schoolteacher to get the class to make some cards from old bits of magazines, cereal packets and company annual reports.

What about the message inside? Typically it might be 'Season's Greetings! We look forward to continuing working with you in the New Year.' Yuck! This leaves too many hostages to fortune. Get the legal guys working on something much more watertight!

Heretofore we have had a commercially viable relationship. Though past performance is no indicator of future success and while we may earnestly endeavour in good faith to continue there is no guarantee that other actors (inter alia, suppliers or customers) may not enter the market with more favourable terms. The sending of this card does not constitute a contract. See you at the Christmas Party.

[*Ned*: This book is coming out at Xmas. Have you had a chance to discuss with your team my ideas for publicity, like L-Vo's Grotto at the Harlequin Shopping Centre? Or me dressed as Father Xmas slaying some elves outside Stevenage station?]

X-Treme Motivator

The highest level to be attained in my new computer game *Grand Theft L-Vo*.

YBM

Young British Motivators. Pretenders to my throne. A clique of self-satisfied charlatans, headed up by Frankie B, who are only in it for the money and glamour, not like me. There's Alan Treacle with his Pull Your Socks Up (PYSU) method. Go on his workshop and he distributes socks of different colours (yellow for relationships, red for career, blue for health). You put them on and pull them up and that way, in turn, each area will improve. Way too simple, Al!

Then there's Brent Fent, with his Power Call. All you have to do first thing every morning is make a 'power call', phoning someone up who is important to you, whether in your personal or your business life. The call has to scare you or you must be sure that it will make a difference to your entire day. That's it. I mean, come on! Where are the merchandising opportunities in that? Though he does seem to have wrung seven books out of it.

Everyone must be amazed by Hillary Pink and his best-selling book, *To Cut a Long Story Short*. Each chapter uses a Spandau Ballet song as a guide to a different aspect of personal development. 'True' helps us take an honest look at ourselves; 'Instinction' encourages us to use our intuition; 'Chant No. 1 (I Don't Need This Pressure On)' helps us cope with STRESS; 'Gold' focuses on wealth mastery; 'Only When You Leave' gives relationship guidance. All in all, it helps the reader leap 'Through the Barricades'. Can you believe it? I only wish I'd thought of it myself. I said as much to Tony Hadley when I saw him in Argos last year.

Yes

The best word in business. That's why I sometimes call it Busn-Yes and Succ-Yes!

Yin and Yang

Earth and Heaven in Chinese. Conceptually it means two opposing but complementary elements – for example, light and dark, North and South, profit and loss, success and failure, Richard & Judy, Ant & Dec, Bill Turnbull and Sian Williams (BBC *Breakfast*). Useful in allocating shared offices or PAs.

Yo-Yoga

Yoga which helps you say Yo to Life, or at least Yo to something. Why not come on one of our Yo-Yoga Yogurt Weekends? We fly to Ibiza from London Luton and it's all Yoga and Yogurt from there. Which flavour yogurt you have depends on your name

See also ALPHABET DIET.

Yo-Yo-Yo-Ga

Yoga with a yo-yo. Only for the advanced and supple SUC-CEEDER. Can help the stressed Chief Executive unwind before facing the board.

Yurt

A portable dwelling from Central Asia. I often stay in one on retreat when I need to be closer to the earth. Lucky I had it when my wife decided I should leave the marital home. I managed to erect it in the car park at Spring Lakes Business Park. My friend Charles lives in it now, since he left his job, family and home to pursue his own Hero's Business Journey. He's reading this book again, before working his way through the daily exercises in my book *Chicken Nuggets for the Soul*.

Zero-Sum Game

If **I** win **you** must lose; or my loss matches your gain. It may be like this in poker but not in life – if you are a SUCCEEDER. For us, it's WIN/WIN/WIN. The winner doesn't take it all (sorry, Abba!) but we can all be winners. We can all achieve our goals – I call it the Hero-Sum Game.

Zoo

A place where animals are kept. Go and study them – to see how BUSINESS is conducted at the basic level. There are negotiations over rewards, territory and status. I recently went 'back-cage' with some gibbons, who reminded me of some hedge fund managers, with their early-morning territory-staking calls, energetic leaping about and fondness for bananas.

 **APPENDICES**

☆ **Acknowledgements**

Obviously I'd like to thank my nephew, Liam, who has done wonders with the SUCCEEDER merchandising operation and was recently asked to speak at the Harpenden Chamber of Commerce. Apparently he's used me as a case study in his GCSE Business Soft Skills dissertation. And Nikki, if you're reading this (I have sent you a copy – you can reimburse me for it later if you like), you know how much you did. Please come back. And to the N-editor, as I call him, thanks for correcting my spelling mistakes. I know you would rather have been working on *Huw Edwards' Welsh Cookery Book* or ghosting *Alastair Darling's Celebrity Confessions*, but maybe that nice girl with brown hair who sits near your office might be available to do my next book.

I'm indebted to Tamma Chookworth, Saskatchewan's leading songstress and answer to Celine Dion by way of Natalie Imbruglia (who used to be in *Neighbours*), for letting me quote her beautiful and aspirational lyrics throughout the book for only a small licence fee, which she has promised to repay if at least thirty-five of you visit her MySpace site (myspace.com/tammachookworth). And a big shout, of course, to *Steve Wright in the Afternoon*!

☆ *Other books by L. Vaughan Spencer*

The Seven Hobbies of Highly Effective People
Overnight Success within a Week
Leadership: Is It OK to Shout?
Irrational Intelligence
Who Moved My Cheeseburger?
Chicken Nuggets for the Soul
Superfood – Superleader?
The Road Less Tarmac'd
Further Along the Road Less Tarmac'd
The Suburban Book of Living and Dyeing
The Tao of Shaving
Me-conomics
What They Don't Teach You at Harvard Infants' School
The Little Book of Big Things
Garden Your Way to the Top
It's Not About the Lettuce
A Child Called 'Oi'
Mind Mopping
The BMX Diaries

Look out for next year's book *Further Along the A to Z of Motivitality*, with entries including:

Bea-Tzu

The Chinese poet-warrior from the 6th century BC. His military philosophy (Win-Git) applies perfectly in today's fast-moving modern business environment (FMMBE). Here are some of his headline thoughts:

How to Win Without Fighting.

Why the Morning Is Best.

A Leader without a Horse Must Walk Many Miles.

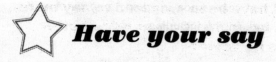 *Have your say*

We welcome your feedback. Fill it in online at thesucceeder.
com/ilovedthebook and you may win your company the
chance of a half-hour consulting session from yours truly!
Early bird special offer: If you do this before 30 November
you may get chance to bid for an hour's consulting!

1. I enjoyed this book because:

It was really good.

It made me think.

It helps me feel close to L-Vo.

2. I will recommend it to others because:

I think it could help a particular colleague.

If my team all had copies we would have so much more
synergy.

Several of my friends are total losers.

3. I am going to come on a Succeeder Weekend because:

I want to meet L. Vaughan Spencer.

I need to know more.

I want to earn my licence to run my own Motivitality
Modules from the comfort of my own home (starter
pack £675 + VAT – more if you are in Guernsey).

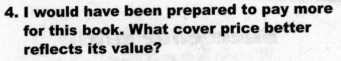

4. I would have been prepared to pay more for this book. What cover price better reflects its value?

£9.99

£11.99

£18.99

5. I have a copy of Frankie B's Life-Changer. I don't need it now, so I will:

Put it in the recycle box.

Send it to his publisher.

Make it into a hat.

Give it to Oxfam.

Burn it.

Use it as toilet paper.

TIE-BREAKER: It is just possible that more than one person (or company) will get all the answers right. If so, here is a tie-breaker. In fewer than 166 words, complete the following:

I love L-Vo because ....

Succeeder Moti-Merchandise

Succeeder Skin Defense

Check out the New Succeeder Manly Moisturiser – for when Business is Getting You Down. Contains: tea tree oil, essence of pig, camomile, quinoa and Zambian mayonnaise. Executive version now downloadable to your iPhone or other digital receiver.

Succeederomatherapeutic Super Soak

Put this in your Buzzness Bath after a long day at work and creativise on BUZZNESS issues. The juniper and grapefruit will help you HOCUS-FOCUS on upcoming business challenges, especially strategy and headcount headaches. Rebalances your energy without drying you out.

Succeeder Skin Survival Cream

For the non-greasy approach to business (with avocado and beetroot). Gets rid of dead cells and micro-activates the others to get excited again.

Succeeder Styling Sludge

Controls your hair without compromising its natural effervescence. This works at the nano level and will leave you confident yet natural.

Rasage de Reussir

Succeedy shave foam to help you get aboard the Shavy Train.

And for the Ladies:

Sista Succeeder She-Shave

For all Lady Zones. A great cushion between your derma-level and that rough old razor. Reduces Femabrasion; non-irritating and surprisingly friendly. Contains porridge.

Three-Letter Acronyms (TLA)

AAA – Animal Archetype Analysis

APP – Authentic Personal Power

ASS – Advanced Seminar on Succeederology

BAP – Bully/Assertive/Pushover

BBT – Biggest Business Triumph

BST – Blood, Sweat and Tears

CCC – Chief Change Commando

CFS – Creative Family Succeeder (house-husband/wife)

CSD – Continuing Succeedy Development

CSO – Chief Succeedy Officer

DDF – Dress-Down Friday

DFV – Dolphin-Focused Visualisation

DLT – 'Don't Like' Test (also Dave Lee Travis, the Hairy Cornflake, who was on BBC Three Counties Radio (Beds, Herts and Bucks) till last year)

ELF – Embedded Lippy Foe

GGM – Give Good Meeting

HBJ – Hero's Business Journey

IPS – Irritating Person Scale

MBS – Management by Smiling

MOO – Motivitality Overcomes Obstacles

MTB – Max the Buffet

NVM – Non-Verbal Messages

OBE – Order of the British Empire

PDB – PerDevBiz (Personal Development and Business are now as one)

PDT – Positive Doing Tool (e.g. P-Move, P-Think, or sorting out your sock drawer)

PMS – Personal Mission Statement

PPF – Post-Post-Feminist

PPP – Peak Performance Performer

PSE – Personal Self-Enhancement

ROI – Return on Investment

ROS – Return on Shavestment

RSL – Rushed Solitary Lunch

SAS – Succeeder Action Squad

SDD – Succeedy Deficit Disorder

SIV – Succeeder Inner Voice

SRW – Succeeder Room Worker

SSS – Succeeder Squad Session

SWD – Succeeder War Dance

TSP – Two-Step Process

UMD – Under-MotivitaliseD

USP – Unique Selling Proposition or Unique Selling Point or Über Succeedy Pants

UTD – Urban Tribal Drumming

YBE – Yesterday's Business Environment

YBM – Young British Motivators

WOM – Word-of-Mouth

Four-or-More-Letter Acronyms (FOMLA)

ERAI – Emotional Risk Assessment Inventory
FMBE – Fast-Moving Business Environment
FMMBE – Fast-Moving Modern Business Environment
FMMGBE – Fast-Moving Modern Global Business Environment
FMMGBME – Fast-Moving Modern Global Business and Management Environment
NFNL – Neither Follower nor Leader
SOSS – Session On Succeeder Strategising

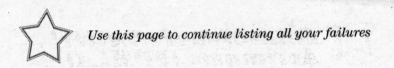

Use this page to continue listing all your failures

*If you have had any, write your **Successes** here*

☆ *The Alphabet Diet*

A – animals, abalone, asparagus, anchovy, Algerian food
B – beef, beetroot, beer, bread, Brie, burger, biscuits,
    banana, beer, Belgian food, brown sauce
C – chicken, cress, cider, carrot, cheese, chips, Chinese
    food, chocolate and chocolate-covered things
D – duck, dressing, dim sum, doughnuts, deep-fried stuff
E – egg, eel, eyes (sheep's), Edam, emu, Ethiopian food
F – fish, fettuccine, focaccia, food, French food, fried food,
    French fries, fricasseed things
G – goose, gherkin, ginger, gravy, Greek food
H – haddock, halibut, horse, hare (jugged), hot food
I – ink (squid), ice cream, imperial mints, Italian food,
    Indian food, iron
J – juice, jackfruit, John Dory, joints of meat, julienne of
    vegetables, Japanese food, jam, Jaffa cakes
K – kale, kipper, KitKat, kangaroo, kedgeree
L – lamb, liver, leek, lettuce, lozenge, luxury mince pies,
    luxury chocolate, luxury taramasalata, Lebanese food
M – mixed veg, Maltesers, meat, mince, melon, mutton,
    McDonald's, milk chocolate
N – nuts, naan bread, noodles, nice things, Nesquik, Nice
    biscuits, neeps in Scotland
O – orange, orange food, oats, olives, ostrich

P – pork, prawn, peach, potato, pickle, pizza, Parmesan, Polish food, protein

Q – quail, Quorn, quick-cook meals

R – radish, Ready Brek, raisins, root vegetables, rabbit, roe, raspberry, Russian food, Ryvita

S – sausages, swordfish, sandwiches, sushi, spaghetti, soya, Stilton, steak, salmon, sautéed anything

T – thyme, trout, tomato, tagliatelle, tempura, tinned food, tuna, Thai food, Tunisian food

U – unagi, undercooked food, underbelly, Ugandan food

V – veal, vegetables, vinegar, Vietnamese food

W – wheat, Weetabix, Worcestershire Sauce, water biscuits, wine, Welsh rarebit and other Welsh food, water, watermelon

X – Xanthan gum (that thing they add to food as a thickener), Xmas cake, Xmas pudding

Y – yogurt, yeast, yolk, yellow food, Yemeni food, yam

Z – zinc, zabaglione, zest of lemon, zebra, zoo animals

Visit thesucceeder.com/alphadiet and add your own suggestions.

☆ *Succeeder Moti-Music*

Certain songs will help you focus on certain issues:

Body language: 'U Can't Touch This', MC Hammer
When you are having difficulty in recruitment:
    'Holding Out for a Hero', Bonnie Tyler
Having Breakfast Meet: 'Pump up the Jam',
    Technotronic
When the going is tough: 'When the Going Gets Tough,
    the Tough Get Going', Billy Ocean

Succeeder Relaxation Tapes

Volume 1: Dolphins in Conversation and Whale Song
Volume 2: Succeeder Silence and Cheese Melting

Succeeder Moti-Mixed Ringtones

Kylie Minogue, 'I Should Be Succeedy'
Phil Collins, 'S-S-S-Succeedio'
Sister Sledge, 'We Are Succeedy'
Gloria Gaynor, 'I Will Succeed'
Steppenwolf, 'Born to Succeed'
Baccara, 'Yes, Sir, I'm Succeedy'
The Commodores, 'Once, Twice, Three Times Succeedy'
The Commodores, 'Succeedy Like Sunday Morning'
Special AKA, 'He's L. Vaughan Spencer' (to tune of 'Free
    Nelson Mandela')

Want to know more about Succeeder Workshops
and buying Motivitalising Merchandise (CDs,
videos and clothing)?

Visit thesucceeder.com now.
Have your credit card ready!

For tip-top training videos, visit Succeed-eVision.com

And next year you can enrol in the Succeeder University!